Rhythm and Folklore
the story of
Zora Neale Hurston

Rhythm and Folklore
the story of
Zora Neale Hurston

Kerrily Sapet

MORGAN REYNOLDS

PUBLISHING

Greensboro, North Carolina

WORLD WRITERS

Charles Dickens
Jane Austen
Ralph Ellison
Stephen King
Robert Frost
O. Henry
Roald Dahl
Jonathan Swift
Leo Tolstoy
Zora Neale Hurston

RHYTHM AND FOLKLORE:
THE STORY OF ZORA NEALE HURSTON
Copyright © 2009 by Kerrily Sapet

Library of Congress Cataloging-in-Publication Data

Sapet, Kerrily, 1972-
    Rhythm and folklore : the story of Zora Neale Hurston / by Kerrily Sapet.
-- 1st ed.
        p. cm.
    Includes bibliographical references and index.
    ISBN-13: 978-1-59935-067-7
    ISBN-10: 1-59935-067-X
    1. Hurston, Zora Neale. 2. Authors, American--20th century--Biography.
3. African American authors--Biography. 4. African American women authors-
-Biography. 5. Folklorists--United States--Biography. 6. African American
women--Southern States--Biography. I. Title.
    PS3515.U789Z87 2008
    813'.52--dc22
    [B]

                                            2008000844

Printed in the United States of America
First Edition

Contents

Zora Neale Hurston
(Library of Congress)

one

Jumping at the Sun

As a young girl, Zora Neale Hurston loved when her mother sent her to the town store. There, she could always find a gathering of men perched on boxes and wooden benches, spinning tales about wily Brer Rabbit or God shaping men out of clay. She liked to listen to their guitars as they sang railroad tunes and strummed the blues.

While Zora's mother waited at home for her sugar and coffee, her daughter soaked up the folktales and the rhythms of the storytellers. About the only thing that could tear her away was her mother's impatient voice, calling young Zora to get home quick or suffer the consequences—a spanking with a switch still fresh with "peach hickories in it."

Those tales would stay with Zora for the rest of her life. She stored away details of the stories, and she began to create her own. She imagined conversations with a bird whose long, colorful tail flowed to the ground and spoke to tall, green pine trees that answered back when the wind blew. She told her mother how she talked with a lake as she walked over it, never getting her feet wet, and how she was able to see all the fish swimming beneath her. When Zora wanted a black horse that her family couldn't afford, she made one up instead. "No one around me knew how often I rode my prancing horse, nor the things I saw in far places," she said years later.

Zora's grandmother called these stories flat-out lies, but Zora's mother indulged her daughter's imagination. Her grandmother's bitter memories of slavery caused her to worry about her granddaughter's free thoughts and speech. "To her my brazenness was unthinkable," Zora wrote.

The world was unprepared for Zora Neale Hurston from the day she was born on January 7, 1891, in the small town of Notasulga, Alabama. January was hog-killing time in Notasulga. In the days before home refrigeration was common, cool winter temperatures kept the fresh meat from spoiling before it could be packed in salt to preserve it. But cold weather did not usually last long in Alabama, and neighbors helped each other slaughter the hogs and preserve the meat in exchange for a portion. Zora's birth wasn't expected for another few weeks and Zora's mother, Lucy, was alone when she gave birth. A man delivering a ham to the house arrived shortly afterwards and helped until the midwife arrived.

Zora was the fifth child in the family. She and her siblings were the second generation of African Americans to be free of slavery. She joined her older brothers, Hezekiah Robert, John Cornelius, and Richard William. Zora also had a sister, Sarah Emmeline, who was her father's favorite.

Zora's father, John, was absent both at her birth and at her naming. John Hurston wanted "plenty more sons, but no more girl babies to wear out shoes and bring in nothing," Zora said. After Zora's birth, Lucy Hurston had three more sons, Clifford Joel, Benjamin Franklin, and Everett Edward.

For the first few years of her life, Zora and her family lived in a small cabin on a white man's plantation. Then her father decided to move the family to Eatonville, Florida, located about six miles from Orlando. The town of Eatonville, formed in 1887 by twenty-seven African Americans, was the first incorporated all-black town in the country. Its first residents had filed papers with the state government for the city to be officially recognized. Completely self-governed by African Americans, Eatonville's proud inhabitants refuted white people's claims that people of color were unable to govern themselves. The only white people in town were temporarily passing through on their way to someplace else. In this town of three hundred people, two schools, and plenty of lakes, Zora grew up surrounded solely by African Americans.

Many of the men and women in Eatonville worked in nearby citrus groves, picking oranges and grapefruit. Women also worked as cooks or maids for white families in the nearby town of Maitland. Zora's father served as Eatonville's mayor for three terms and also as the town minister. He was known for his bravery, powerful leadership, and lyrical, poetic preaching, which Zora loved.

Family legend told how John Hurston once "cold-conked" a mule with his fist. He also could swing "bales of cotton like suitcases," Zora wrote, and swim Lake Maitland from end to end. "We had seen him bring down bears and panthers

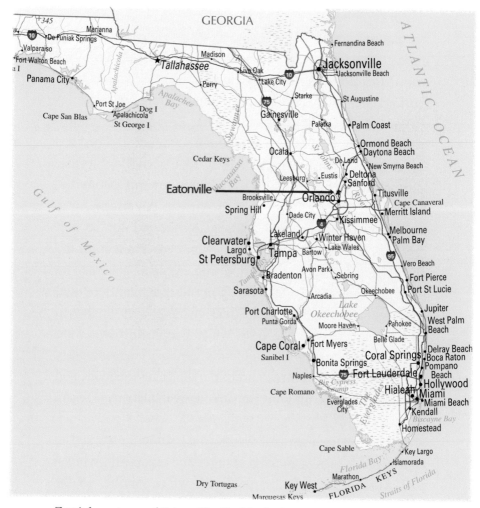

Zora's hometown of Eatonville, Florida, is about six miles north of Orlando. *(Courtesy of the National Atlas)*

with his gun, and chin the bar more times than any man in competing distance," she added. "All that part was just fine with me. But I was Mama's child."

Although Zora was awed by her father's strength, she often was at odds with him. She was spirited, highly inquisitive, and at times belligerent. Zora's father complained that in a

Children playing in Eatonville, Florida *(Library of Congress)*

white-dominated world his daughter would be hanged before she was grown. He warned that someday Lucy would "suck sorrow for not beating my temper out of me before it was too late," Zora once said.

The world outside of Eatonville was harsher than Zora realized. Although it had been nearly thirty years since the Civil War ended, both the North and the South continued to reel from the effects. Four million freed slaves could now marry, raise families, find paid work on farms and in cities, and save money to buy farms of their own. Despite these new rights, many whites across the country believed that African Americans were unable to think for themselves, plan for the future, and make intelligent political choices.

The newly formed Ku Klux Klan, a white supremacist group protesting slaves' newfound freedoms, lynched thousands of black people.

In the 1880s and 1890s southern states continued to separate the races. In 1896 the United States Supreme Court ruled that states could require racial segregation in public places, such as schools, as long as these facilities were equal. This decision culminated from a court case named *Plessy v. Ferguson*, and became known as the separate but equal doctrine. White and black Americans had separate schools, railroad and trolley cars, theaters, parks, beauty shops, and even drinking fountains. This legalized discrimination spread into the North as well. In theory the separation provided equal opportunities, but in reality it did not.

Southerner Amanda Smith Jemand wrote:

> No honest man will say we get equal if separate [railroad or trolley] cars. In the drug stores we can buy poison, but not a five-cent glass of soda water. We can mix bread with our hands; it is good enough to go into their stomachs, but not a penny roll can we eat in their restaurants. We can sleep in their houses, in their beds, by their sides as long as we are servants; but go into some public hostelry with money to buy our lodging in a separate room and bed, immediately we have developed a case of leprosy.

States and towns passed laws segregating every public area from transportation to hospitals to restaurants. "Whites Only" and "No Colored" signs dotted towns in the South and were not unknown in the North. The laws became known as Jim Crow laws. While historians still debate the true origin of the term, most agree that Jim Crow was not a real person, but instead a character in a song sung in the 1830s

An African American man drinks from a segregated water cooler in the Jim Crow South. *(Library of Congress)*

about a black man. White performer Thomas "Daddy" Rice imitated the dress, talk, and walk of African Americans, blackening his face with burned cork for his shows. His song "Jump Jim Crow," portraying an elderly black man with a disability, became popular. Many white people, both in the North and the South, left such performances—called minstrel shows—with distorted images of African Americans. Over time, the term Jim Crow came to refer to segregation as a government-sanctioned system. Segregation limited every aspect of life—where black people could live, study, work, play, worship, travel, and be buried.

Yet Eatonville sheltered Zora from all of this. Just through the trees from her house was Joe Clarke's store with its storytelling porch. In her yard full of orange, grapefruit,

Joe Clark's store in the 1940s *(Courtesy of Zora Neale Hurston Collection, George A. Smathers Libraries, University of Florida, Department of Special Collections)*

tangerine, and guava trees, she chased away alligators and grew up strong. She loved the baking hot Florida sunshine and being outside. A tomboy, she had the reputation of being "the one girl who could take a good pummeling without running home to tell." Lucy and John Hurston urged her to be more ladylike and to play with the dolls she got for Christmas. Instead Zora made her dolls get into fights. By New Year's the dolls leaked the sawdust they were stuffed with.

Zora and her brothers and sisters lived in an eight-room house on five acres of land. The family had a huge garden of vegetables and fruits. They had so many hens that the children sometimes boiled eggs in a large iron kettle then lay in the front yard, eating until they were full. Between chicken, fresh vegetables, and plenty of homemade cornbread, the children had their fill of food. They lobbed the leftover hard-boiled eggs at each other like hand grenades. They also had plenty of company with each other as playmates.

As a former country school teacher, Zora's mother Lucy was strongly committed to her children's education. She gathered her children each night in her bedroom for extra lessons in grammar and arithmetic. Zora learned to read before she was of school age. Her mother was the biggest influence in her early life. A tiny woman, Lucy Hurston was intelligent and steely tough. She quietly, but tenaciously, stood up to her husband who frequently was away and often with other women. Lucy advised her daughter to "Jump at de sun. We might not land on the sun, but at least we would get off the ground."

But Zora's reading enraged her father. He forbade her to read novels, believing them to be the devil's work. Defying him, Zora voraciously read everything she could find, including poetry. When eight-year-old Zora announced at dinner one evening that she planned to become a poet some day her father thundered an angry response. "It is my understanding that poets are low-living creatures with no God in their hearts and no Bible in their hands," he yelled. "If you want to do something, be a missionary!" Zora fled the kitchen. Their frequent arguments usually ended with a whipping or with John Hurston chasing his daughter out the door. Zora's mother often came to her defense.

"Zora is my young'un, and Sarah is yours," Lucy told her husband. "You leave her alone. I'll tend to her when I figger she needs it."

Zora's mother's support paid off. Her daughter's reading ability so impressed two white women visiting Zora's school that they requested Zora visit them at a local hotel where they were staying. As they fed Zora stuffed dates and candied ginger, Zora tasted a glimpse of life beyond Eatonville. Afterwards the women sent her gifts of clothes and an even more precious treasure—a box of books. Before that, Zora's family library had consisted of a Bible. Finding other books to read had often proved difficult. Nearby towns forbade African Americans from using their libraries, and Eatonville had no library of its own. Now Zora could read Grimm's fairy tales, Greek and Roman myths, Norse legends, and other tales. Through these books, she discovered other worlds beyond the gate in her front yard.

At times Zora's mother found her intelligent and spunky daughter exasperating. Zora was spanked for repeating gossip and for sitting on the gatepost and calling to white travelers driving down the road, "Don't you want me to go a piece of the way with you?" Despite the times when Lucy reined her daughter in, Zora was her mother's child and never forgot it. Lucy let her free-spirited daughter be herself.

One day when Zora was about seven years old, four visions suddenly appeared in her mind. She saw herself as an orphan, wandering cold and homeless. Next, she saw herself hurrying to catch a train; she was seeking peace and not finding it. Third, Zora pictured a shabby house in need of a new coat of white paint. Inside that house lay torture, but she knew she had to go into it. Last, Zora saw a large house with two women, one older, one younger. Both women stood by a beautiful vase of flowers. It was here that Zora would know peace and love. As a child Zora never told anyone about these four visions. She feared these detailed scenes foretold future events in her life. Little did Zora know, but the first picture was on the horizon.

Zora's mother had gotten a persistent cold in her chest and had taken to her bed. For weeks Lucy had been getting thinner, following her sister's recent death. Now, on September 18, 1904, she called thirteen-year-old Zora into her room. Near death, Lucy gave her daughter instructions. She told Zora not to take the pillow from under her head and not to cover the clock or the mirror with a cloth upon her death. These strange requests flaunted three established rituals of death in Eatonville. Lucy Hurston was symbolically rejecting the folklore of the village.

People in Eatonville, as in many rural communities at the time, believed that when a person died their spirit might haunt survivors. They removed the pillow from under a person's head so that the dying process would not be prolonged. They also covered mirrors to avoid any reflection of the corpse, otherwise the spirit would be able to attach permanently to the glass. They covered the clock because it would forever cease its ticking if a person looked at it when dying. Survivors practiced these rituals to cope with their feelings of loss. But Lucy Hurston didn't want any part of the rituals. She charged her daughter with the burden of preventing them.

As the sun set, Zora noticed many women going into her mother's room and staying there. She too went in, joining her father, who stood over his wife. It was time for Zora to carry out her promise and prevent the rituals, but she was no match for the women and her father. John Hurston physically held his daughter back from carrying out her mother's last request. Crushed at having let her mother down Zora wrote, "I was old before my time with grief of loss, of failure, or remorse of failure." My mother "had felt that I could and would carry out her wishes, and I had not. And then in that sunset time, I failed her. It seemed as she died that the sun went down on purpose to flee away from me."

Zora would agonize for years over being unable to fulfill this promise. Lucy Hurston's death signaled the end of a phase in Zora's life. Her world forever changed. "That hour began my wanderings, not so much in geography, but in time. Then not so much in time as in spirit," Zora wrote.

As her family huddled together absorbing the shock, Zora wondered about her father's feelings. "I have often wished I had been old enough at the time to look into Papa's heart that night," she wrote. "If I could know what that moment meant to him, I could have set my compass toward him and been sure."

John Hurston did the best he could, but more of the household responsibilities fell on Zora's shoulders. John's heart was broken, as was Zora's, but he alienated his daughter still further by his inability to comfort her and to express his pain. Zora's life was adrift, and her father would fail to pull her back.

Instead, Zora's father sent her off to boarding school in Jacksonville, Florida, along with her brother Bob and sister

An undated photo of Zora as a young woman *(Courtesy of the Stetson Kennedy Foundation Collection, Zora Neale Hurston Collection, George A. Smathers Libraries, University of Florida, Department of Special Collections)*

Sarah. Miserable, Sarah returned home to an unpleasant shock. In February of 1905, within five months of their mother's death, John Hurston had married his former mistress, twenty-year-old Mattie Oxedine. To make matters worse, Mattie had no tolerance for her new stepchildren. She kicked Sarah out of the house and had John beat his daughter with a buggy whip for commenting on their marriage. When Zora heard this news she was livid and wanted revenge. Sarah however landed on her feet. She fled and soon married, settling near St. Petersburg, Florida.

Life for Zora continued to be difficult. Along with her family troubles, Jacksonville was different from her hometown. The day she arrived for school, Zora said, was "the very day I became colored." Unlike all-black Eatonville, 135 miles away, Jacksonville was segregated. Where before she was "everybody's Zora" and could walk into a store and receive a bag of crackers or a piece of candy, here she was anonymous. "Jacksonville made me know that I was a little colored girl," Zora said.

Zora longed for her hometown and her mother. "I was deprived of the loving pine [her favorite tree], the lakes, the wild violets in the woods, and the animals I used to know," she wrote. "No more holding down first base on the team with my brothers and their friends. Just a jagged hole where my home used to be."

John Hurston decided not to pay for Zora's schooling. Zora paid her own tuition by scrubbing stairs and helping in the kitchen after classes. On Saturdays she cleaned the pantry. The highlight of her year was when she won the citywide spelling bee. Her prize was a Bible and an atlas. She drank her fill of lemonade and ate so much cake that she joked she could feel it coming through her skin. But the year ended sourly for Zora. Her teachers told her to stay until her father sent for her, but he never did.

"I kept looking out of the windows so that I could see Papa when he came up the walk to the office," she said. "But nobody came for me. Weeks passed, and then a letter came. Papa said that the school could adopt me . . . it was crumbling news for me." The administration paid her way home by boat, where a kindly waiter kept her fed.

Zora's homecoming was miserable. Unwanted by her step-mother and never sure of her standing with her father, the situation grew steadily worse. John Hurston's new wife got her way when she demanded that all four of the youngest children, Zora included, be placed in relatives' homes. The next five years Zora describes as haunted.

"I was shifted from house to house of relatives and friends and found comfort nowhere . . ." she wrote. "I was miserable, and no doubt made others miserable around me, because they could not see what was the matter with me." Zora led her life clothed in hand-me-downs and eating hit-or-miss meals in a series of different homes.

After Zora left her father's home, she literally disappeared from public record. Little is known about this time in her life. A black woman could disappear relatively easily at the time. If a girl or woman was not legally linked to a man as a daughter or wife, she wasn't officially counted. Few black women owned property. They also were not allowed to vote, although black men were given the right to vote in 1870 with the passage of the Fifteenth Amendment to the Bill of Rights. In the early twentieth century both black and white women still clamored and fought for the right to vote.

At fourteen years old, Zora wasn't considered too young to work. Her relatives expected her to earn some of her keep. In the early 1900s more than 40 percent of black women over the age of ten were working. Zora held several jobs as a maid, but few of her positions lasted long. She quickly got bored or was fired for not being humble enough. Zora also refused to submit to the sexual advances of her employers. She found a job working as a receptionist in a doctor's office. She was good at her job, and the doctor encouraged her to become a nurse. However, Zora longed for the world of books and learning. She envied those who were able to go to school. In these miserable and lonely years Zora said she discovered, "Poverty smells like death. People can be slave ships in shoes . . ."

For a brief time Hurston returned to "her father's house, which was no longer my home." The reunion was short lived. One day a violent fight erupted between Hurston and her stepmother.

"She called me a sassy, impudent helper, announcing that she was going to take me down a buttonhole lower, and threw a bottle at my head," Hurston said. "The bottle came sailing slowly through the air and missed me easily. She never should have missed." During the spitting, kicking, and scratching fight that resulted, Hurston supposedly threw a hatchet that struck the door behind Mattie, who slumped to the floor in exhaustion and fear. When Hurston's stepmother threatened to have her arrested, John Hurston stepped in and refused. Even so Hurston left home once again. Soon after, Mattie moved out and the couple divorced.

Shortly after the knockdown brawl with her stepmother Hurston left Florida to live with her brother Bob in Tennessee.

Bob needed Hurston to help his wife with their three children while he studied at Meharry Medical College. The college was one of two institutions in the country that trained black doctors. It had opened after the American Civil War to treat the health conditions of freed slaves who hadn't received medical attention for years. In exchange for Hurston's help, Bob promised to pay for her schooling. Hurston leaped at the chance. Hurston was leaving behind frustration and defeat. Later she vividly remembered the red sunset she viewed from the train that evening. "There have been other suns that set in significance for me, but that sun! It was a bookmark in the pages of a life," she wrote.

Soon after Hurston arrived at her brother's house, Bob decided he needed her to stay home with the children. She wouldn't be able to enroll in high school right away. Although disappointed, Hurston adored the children and living with family. Soon they all moved to Memphis, Tennessee where Bob set up his medical practice. Hurston lived with Bob's family for two years, daily growing more impatient for schooling, and feeling more like a live-in maid and nanny. With her independent spirit, she also didn't appreciate her older brother's rules. Again another of Hurston's visions had come true. She had boarded a train seeking peace and love and had not found it. In 1914 Hurston moved on, still hoping to finish high school. For a brief time she lived with her brother John Cornelius and his wife Blanche in Jacksonville, Florida, but she soon moved out.

Sometime in the next year many people believe Hurston may have secretly married. There is no marriage record but people who have studied her life, along with some of her family members, suggest that she married an abusive man and that her deep love was betrayed, just like in her vision. She mentions in her autobiography that her third vision came true in these years. The vision involved a shabby white house—torture and pain lay within, but she had to go inside. But all of these are questions, lost due to time and due to the fact that Hurston kept portions of her life private.

It's difficult to pin down dates in Hurston's life during this time. Her birth records have not survived. Throughout her life she gave different dates to impress on people either her youth or her age. She claimed her birth date to be anywhere from 1898 to 1903. Census records and one of her family members suggest she was born in 1891.

By 1915 she had joined a traveling theater troupe as a lady's maid to the group's lead singer Miss M. Zora cared for Miss M.'s clothes and cosmetics and helped the singer dress. For this she received $10.00 a week, equivalent to about $160.00 today. She had boarded the train to join the troupe with a suitcase containing a comb, a brush, and toothpaste. She stuffed the suitcase with newspaper to keep her meager possessions from rattling around inside. The only African American and southerner, Hurston's colorful expressions amused the group. She might call someone a "hog-nosed, gator-faced . . . puzzle-gutted, camel-backed . . . knock-kneed, razor-legged, box-ankled, shovel-footed, unmated so and so . . ." The troupe's tenor, a man educated in music, opera, and theater, lent Hurston books to read. She was thrilled. Her eighteen months of traveling with the troupe soothed the hurts of Hurston's past years. The group's members gently teased her and stuffed her with Coca-Cola and ice cream. She lived in a diverse community, visiting cities in Maryland, Pennsylvania, Connecticut, and

Zora around 1916 *(Courtesy of the Stetson Kennedy Foundation Collection,
Zora Neale Hurston Collection, George A. Smathers Libraries, University of Florida,
Department of Special Collections)*

Virginia, and seeing part of a larger world. A career could fill up "the empty holes left by love," Hurston observed. When Miss M. married and left the stage, she gave Hurston some money and encouraged her to go back to school. By the time the troupe finished its last performance, Hurston had decided to follow her dream of attending high school and college.

By working with the troupe, "I had loosened up in every joint and expanded in every direction," Hurston wrote. "Working with these people I had been sitting by a warm fire for a year and a half and gotten used to the feel of peace. I took a firm grip on the only weapon I had—hope, and set my feet."

two

Drenched in the Light

n 1917 Hurston arrived in Baltimore, Maryland, finally planning to enroll in high school. At the time a high school education was virtually unavailable to African Americans, especially in the South. While the population of African Americans was nearly 11 million, there were only sixty-seven black public high schools, with fewer than 20,000 students. African Americans met great challenges in public schools. Only during the years following the Civil War were public schools established for African Americans. Typically they were underfunded; students had fewer books and were crowded into ramshackle buildings.

As always Hurston was short of money and family support. She took a job as a waitress at a restaurant where meals cost a quarter, and customers tipped her in nickels. She made little money and resented having to fend off men's sexual advances. When appendicitis forced her to have surgery her plans were further put on hold.

Once Hurston recovered, she again tried her hand at waitressing, but this time on her own terms. She opened a shop in her house with her housemate Martha Tucker. She and Martha sold cigarettes, soft drinks, and sundaes out of their restaurant, called Hurston and Tucker.

Soon Hurston's sister Sarah moved to Baltimore with her husband. Sarah also opened up a restaurant in her house in the same neighborhood. The sisters' lives diverged, yet they enjoyed being close to each other. But Hurston grew increasingly frustrated waiting for school. When business floundered, she decided to circumvent one small rule. Maryland laws provided free admission to public school for all black youths between six and twenty years of age. By 1917 Hurston was twenty-six years old. She shaved ten years off her age, declaring her birth date to be in 1901. No one in town knew her history, and she could pass for much younger than she actually was. In September 1917 Hurston enrolled in evening classes at the college prep school called Morgan Academy in Baltimore.

Hurston owned one dress, one change of underwear, and one pair of tan oxford shoes. A rough working girl, with big bones, high cheekbones and freckles, she had dark brown eyes that shone with intelligence. Hurston's voice was striking and rich. Soon school officials arranged part-time jobs to ease her path through school.

None of Hurston's classmates suspected her age, but the teachers relied on her maturity. English and history teachers asked her to fill in for them when they were absent. Once she substituted for a teacher for an entire month.

Hurston's most influential teacher was Dwight O.W. Holmes. He understood her past, complimented her work, and directed her sentences and feet forward. His help empowered her. Hurston thrived in school, graduating in June 1918.

"This was my world, I said to myself, and I shall be in it, and surrounded by it, if it is the last thing I do on God's green dirt-ball," Hurston wrote.

While Hurston finished her initial schooling, a great migration north occurred. Within a period of a few years 300,000 African Americans left the South for northern cities. Most people migrated from Georgia, Virginia, and the Carolinas. The North had symbolized freedom since the Civil War. Now the North offered economic freedom as well. From 1915 to 1916 the South had suffered several economic woes. The lands were plagued by droughts, floods, and boll weevils, insects that destroyed crops. Wages were already low, but black workers in the South earned one-third less money for performing the same tasks as other workers. Their housing was also substandard. Many black families lived in old slave cabins or in shacks built on the crumbling foundations of slave quarters. Many people migrated north because there was a labor shortage as well. In 1917 the United States had become involved in World War I and workers were needed to fill soldier's jobs.

The North had a better reputation. It offered better wages and housing, a refuge from poverty, and fewer Jim Crow laws. But the North was no promised land. Segregation was still customary. Men were still lynched. Domestic violence still occurred against women. The Ku Klux Klan had undergone a period of nationwide growth. By 1925 its members totaled 5 million. Even so, migrating offered the promise of hope. It contributed to a sense of self assertion and independence.

Hurston wrote:

> And black men's feet learned roads. Some said goodbye
> cheerfully . . . others fearfully, with terrors of unknown dangers
> in their mouths . . . others in their eagerness of distance said
> nothing. The daybreak found them gone. The wind said North.
> Trains said North. The tides and tongues said North, and men
> moved like the great herds before the glaciers.

Hurston's father was one of the people who traveled north.
He moved to Memphis, without his wife Mattie. Tragically
though, while he was crossing railroad tracks in his car, a
train crashed into his vehicle. At fifty-seven years old John

Because of poor living conditions in the rural South, many African
Americans began migrating north to find better jobs and housing.
(Library of Congress)

Hurston died. Never especially close to her father, Hurston did not attend his funeral. She was busy plotting her next move. With her friends' and teachers' encouragement she set her sights on college.

Hurston moved to Washington, D.C., in hopes of attending Howard University. America's largest black university, Howard was founded in 1867. Located about three miles from the White House, it had a reputation for scholastic excellence, requiring four years of Latin and two years of Greek. In essence it was the black equivalent of Harvard, at a time when only 2,132 black people were enrolled in college across the United States. Hurston was accepted, but first she needed to attend Howard Academy, as Morgan had not fully prepared her for the university. One teacher at the academy recognized Hurston's potential calling her a "rough edged diamond." Hurston earned her diploma from Howard Academy

Howard University circa 1910 *(Library of Congress)*

in May of 1919 and planned to enter Howard University in the fall as an English major.

In the meantime the university's dean, William Pickens, found Hurston a job. As she had no money and no family to support her, for a short time Hurston lived with a doctor and his wife. She did housework and helped the doctor's wife who had a broken hip. In return they paid for Hurston's tuition and gave her two dollars a week. They also didn't mind her interest in their library. In her spare time Hurston memorized poems as if they would run away from her if she didn't read them fast enough.

Hurston's Howard years were busy ones. She attended classes in the morning, worked until after 8:00 pm, then studied into the night. She held a variety of jobs. For a while she worked part-time as a manicurist in a barber shop near the White House. Many of her clients were senators and congressmen. Knowing Hurston was a student, they left her generous tips and sometimes helped her study her lessons as they chatted. On average she earned between twelve to fifteen dollars a week. Hurston also waitressed at the exclusive Cosmos Club frequented by U.S. President Theodore Roosevelt and British author Rudyard Kipling. At other times Hurston also worked as a maid for wealthy black families. Surrounded by money and elegance, Hurston soon became stylish. She draped herself in long dresses, dramatic colors, and fancy hats, even though her new clothes strained her meager income.

Hurston enjoyed her days at Howard, especially with romantic prospects on the horizon. In 1920, when she was twenty-nine years old, she met Herbert Sheen. A fellow Howard student, Sheen was from Decatur, Illinois. As children of ministers

A stylish Hurston stands with a ukulele on the campus of Howard University. *(Courtesy of Yale Collection of American Literature, Beinecke Rare Book and Manuscript Library)*

they had much in common, despite the fact that Sheen was six years younger. As a hotel waiter, he also was working his way through school. A romance between them quickly developed and continued even when Sheen moved to New York in 1921 to work for a physician.

Despite her busy schedule, Hurston found time to work, study, date, and lose herself in books. Hurston's English teachers encouraged her to apply for entrance into the campus literary club Stylus. Students entered into a competition to obtain membership. Headed by one of her professors, Alain Locke, the club consisted of nineteen members. Hurston quickly gained entry, despite the fact that Locke did not like women writers. Hurston flourished at Stylus and enjoyed marathon literary discussions. These experiences enthralled her and helped spur her writing career.

In 1921 she published her first story in *Stylus* magazine. The story was titled "John Redding Goes to Sea." The plot told of a young dreamer who leaves his rural village to sail off to new horizons. Beaten down by circumstances, John Redding is eventually killed. In some ways the themes of the story echo those of Hurston's life.

Hurston also dabbled in poetry, writing the melancholy poem "Home" when Eatonville's pull tugged at her heart. Hurston also wrote about love in a classic southern black dialect called Gullah. Gullah is a Creole blend of English and African languages that developed in the isolated coastal plantations of the South. The coastal areas from South Carolina to Georgia are still rich in Gullah culture today. Today Gullah storytellers still weave their tales, artists coil baskets from sweetgrass, and cooks create seafood stews called Low Country Boils and fragrant sweet potato pies. This rich culture swirled around Hurston as she struggled to find her literary voice. Her poems were still stiff. However in 1922 she published three poems in the *Negro World* news-paper. It was the first and final time her poetry would ever be published nationally.

Hurston had entered Howard four years earlier, but because of her continuous need to work, she had only completed about one and a half years of college. Her grades were inconsistent; she aced the classes she enjoyed and failed the classes she didn't, such as physical education. In 1923 next to everyone's photos in the university yearbook each student wrote their personal mottos. Amidst all of the clichés stands Hurston's: "I have a heart with room for every joy."

Hurston in Washington, D.C. (*Courtesy of the Stetson Kennedy Foundation Collection, Zora Neale Hurston Collection, George A. Smathers Libraries, University of Florida, Department of Special Collections*)

Soon Hurston wrote another story. Titled "Drenched in Light" the tale tells about a day in the life of Isie Watts, a poor young black girl who lives life to the fullest. Isie sits on a fence post and begs rides from passing white travelers, just like Hurston did as a child. At the end of one ride the white traveler comments, "I would like just a little of her sunshine to soak into my soul. I would like that a lot." Despite Isie being poor and black she is drenched in light, while Hurston's white character suffers from the absence of such joy. Hurston's professor recommended it to Charles Johnson, the publisher of *Opportunity: A Journal of Negro Life*. The magazine served as a forum to introduce new African American writers and

Charles Johnson *(Library of Congress)*

their work. Johnson snapped up Hurston's story and published it in 1924. It was her first nationally published story. "Drenched in the Light" affirmed her memories of Eatonville as a place of peace and happiness.

Johnson encouraged Hurston to come to New York so she could meet and work with other talented writers. His suggestion appealed to Hurston. After another illness she was running even lower on money. She couldn't afford the luxury of paying tuition. It was time for her to move on; New York seemed to be the best destination. By now she had a firmer grip on who she was and what she wanted in life.

Just as Hurston set her feet towards New York, Herbert Sheen's plans to study with a doctor fell through. For a time Sheen played the piano in jazz combos to earn money. After Hurston traveled to New York, Sheen headed to the University of Chicago. He earned his bachelor's degree and entered medical school. Although they were separated by distance, both understood that one day in the future they would marry. As an aspiring writer, Hurston also planned to finish her education. At the time when she was hoping to become a writer, three out of ten African Americans couldn't sign their names. Hurston had $1.50 in her purse and carried most of her belongings in her bag, along with several manuscripts. Hurston had "no job, no friends, and a lot of hope." It was a situation in which she thrived.

three

Harlem and Hope

Hurston arrived in New York City in the first week of January 1925. She was once again jumping at the sun, just as her mother had once encouraged her to do. The first thing Hurston did was to go to Charles Johnson's office. One month earlier he had published her short story "Drenched in the Light." As the editor of *Opportunity: A Journal of Negro Life,* Johnson had launched his magazine in 1923. It was the magazine of the National Urban League, a group founded in 1910 to help blacks migrating from the south adjust to the problems of living in northern cities. They worked to improve housing and employment conditions. Even so these efforts did little for those at the bottom of the heap. Shortly after President Woodrow Wilson's inauguration in 1913 he signed an executive order segregating dining rooms and restrooms used by federal employees in Washington, D.C. His decision would stand for the next twenty-five years.

Johnson's magazine expressed what was dubbed "New Negro" philosophy. "New Negros" refused to accept a subordinate role in society. The magazine explored racial issues and promoted gradual integration and diplomacy between the races. Johnson counted on the skills of writers like Hurston to prove that the races were culturally equal.

At the time there were two other leading black magazines: *The Crisis* and *The Messenger.* W. E. B. Du Bois founded *The Crisis* in 1910 when he organized the National Association for the Advancement of Colored People (NAACP). The NAACP aimed to abolish all legalized segregation, implement equal education for children, and to put an end to racial violence. Du Bois's magazine decried racial injustice and violence. He encouraged direct acts to prevent racism and sought out writings untainted by racial stereotypes, such as folklore. This was Hurston's element. However different the three magazines appeared, each served as a forum to encourage black writers and artists. It meant for Hurston that the time was ripe for her work.

Johnson encouraged Hurston to stay in New York. He often helped young writers onto their feet, finding them places to stay, providing them with phone numbers and personal connections, and offering them important advice. For Hurston he did the same. He even helped her to find a series of odd jobs to pay her way. She moved into an apartment in Harlem with three roommates. The trio gave Hurston a comfortable couch to sleep on, free food, and company. Hurston enjoyed the friendly welcome. Johnson's wife often invited Hurston to dinner, paying for her carfare back and forth.

Each day Hurston passed the Tree of Hope, an old elm tree and one of Harlem's talismans. Many people rubbed

W. E. B. Du Bois

the tree's bark to give them luck and success. The tree also served as a meeting place and conversational grapevine about job openings in the arts.

Black New Yorkers had built Harlem in defiance of discrimination. African Americans had lived in Manhattan for two hundred years. Slowly they migrated from the tip of the

An aerial view of Harlem, New York, in the early twentieth century
(*Library of Congress*)

island to uptown looking for better accommodations. By
1900 Harlem was overbuilt with new apartments. The Civil
Rights Act of 1866 prohibited racial discrimination when selling housing, but the law had little teeth and wasn't strongly
enforced. But with so many empty buildings and apartments
in Harlem, developers seized upon the idea of opening the
housing up to African Americans. By the beginning of World
War I in 1917 Harlem was occupied primarily by black citi-
zens. By the end of the war, after the steady migration of
southern black workers had come north for industrial jobs,
more than 100,000 people made Harlem a city within a city. It
was the cultural capital of black America, with black policemen, businessmen, doctors, lawyers, and judges. Many even

said it was the black capital of the world, with black people swarming in from different states, islands in the Caribbean, and Africa. By 1930, 200,000 people called Harlem home. "If my race can make Harlem," one man commented, "Good Lord, what can't it do."

Others held similar views. One folk saying was, "I'd rather be a lamppost in Harlem than governor of Georgia."

African American poet Langston Hughes perhaps said it best. I "was in love with Harlem long before I got there."

Soon Hurston submitted two stories to an *Opportunity* magazine contest. One entry, a play entitled *Spunk,* illustrated Florida folklife. The other entry, "Color Struck," told the story of a woman self conscious about her dark skin. Each entry took second place in their category. She won a much needed $70.00 in prize money. On a May evening in 1925 Hurston attended an awards dinner, held at a ritzy restaurant on Fifth Avenue. Hurston and the other guests dined on chicken, peas, and mashed potatoes. Often such dinners were at odds with the winning authors' situations. A year earlier the young black poet Langston Hughes had used up most of his $40.00 prize money to pay for his train ticket to New York City.

Only five months after knocking on *Opportunity's* door, Hurston was being hailed as one of the new prominent talents in the black arts. She used the dinner to make contacts, impressing those who met her, and making friendships that would help further her career.

Hurston's quick mind caught the attention of Annie Nathan Meyer. A novelist, Meyer also was one of the founders of Barnard College, the women's equivalent of Columbia University. Shortly after their meeting at the awards dinner,

Meyer arranged for Hurston to study at Barnard. Hurston's admission alone was quite an achievement. Only 13,000 black students attended college, less than three hundred of them at white schools. Hurston would cross Barnard's color barrier, being the college's first black student. Hurston was undaunted.

"I had the same feeling at Barnard that I did at Howard, only more so." she wrote. "I felt that I was highly privileged and determined to make the most of it. I did not resolve to be a grind, however, to show the white folks that I had brains."

Meyer helped Hurston find the $320.00, equivalent to about three thousand dollars today, that she needed for tuition. In the fall of 1925 Hurston enrolled as a transfer student. Barnard proved to be a continuous financial struggle. Hurston had classes three days a week from the morning until five o'clock in the afternoon. She searched for a job that matched her schedule. She also owed an additional $117.00 for books, and the required gym outfit, tennis racket, and a golf outfit. She had eleven cents to her name.

Hurston's search for funds over the next few years required her to look for patrons. Hurston's relationships with white patrons were a complex pattern of dance steps. She signed her first letters to them as either "Most sincerely your humble and obedient servant" or "Devotedly, your pickanniny." She won their financial support with a bittersweet humor. After Hurston received the money, she often dropped such submissive endearments, instead signing letters less humbly.

Before the turn of the century black poet Paul Laurence Dunbar wrote, "We wear the mask that grins and lies. It hides our cheeks and shades our eyes. This debt we pay to human guile. With torn and bleeding hearts we smile . . ." Hurston was learning to wear that same mask, hiding her true feelings at times, to achieve what she needed.

Another one of the friendships Hurston had made at the *Opportunity* dinner was with the popular novelist and contest judge Fannie Hurst. When she discovered Hurston's need for money and a steady job, she hired her as a live-in secretary and proofreader. Hurst ignored the fact that Hurston neither typed well, nor was particularly detail oriented or prompt. Unimpressed by her employer's fame, Hurston rushed ahead of Hurst's thoughts, impatiently interjecting her own ideas. Hurst eventually fired Hurston as a secretary because she was tired of "shorthand . . . short of legiblity" and filing that was "a game of find the thimble." Hurst however kept Hurston on as a chauffeur and companion for another year. Although only five years separated the women, both lied about their age and each assumed the age gap was wider. Their relationship was more personal than professional. Hurston had "the gift of walking into hearts," Hurst once said.

Hurston encountered little overt prejudice because she was identified as contributing to the cultural movement called the Harlem Renaissance. She was a "New Negro," with her presence and her achievements illustrating the absurdity of second-class citizenship for black people. The Harlem Renaissance was bound between the armistice ending World War I and the Great Depression. During this time period Harlem was the center of a great upsurge of African American literature, music, art, and theater. Between 1919 and 1930 more black writers published works than in any decade prior to 1960. Many of those artists who took part in this flowering had parents and grandparents who had witnessed

Fannie Hurst *(Courtesy of AP Images)*

slavery. The movement was characterized by racial pride as its artistic achievements challenged pervasive racism.

Large numbers of incredibly talented African Americans flocked to New York in the 1920s and participated in a literary uprising that forever changed black literature. Previously people had seen literature about black people written by whites. These tales stemmed from the interpretations of plantation poetry, based on slave quarter sing-a-longs and stories. Now, because of the increased assertion of black independence, historical and cultural forces were converging. People were no longer content to only hear white versions. They wanted the authentic and true.

After Hurston's splashy debut at the *Opportunity* contest dinner, she met people quickly, especially impressing those in black cultural circles. Even though Hurston had only published a little yet, it was in the right places. Johnson had designed these contests and dinners for people just like Hurston. He was certain that New York was ready to take Hurston seriously, by supporting her and cultivating her talent. Hurston's new social circles were a far cry from her life at Howard in Washington, D.C. There, except for her schooling, she was one of the multitudes of black women working as a public service employee. Hurston had traded in manicuring nails for lending her voice to feisty literary dinners at Johnson's house. She attended lectures, plays, parties, and poetry readings.

Hurston quickly earned a reputation in New York for spinning funny stories about life in Eatonville. The storytelling skills from Joe Clarke's porch had sunk into Hurston's soul, and people gathered around her as she wove her tales. With her wit and mimicry, she impressed, amused, and charmed her listeners. "Almost before you knew it, she had gotten into a story," said fellow writer Arna Bontemps.

When Hurston was present, she often became the life of the party. She loved dressing flamboyantly with lots of bangles and beads. She and Langston Hughes soon became fast friends. Hurston "was certainly the most amusing of all the Harlem Renaissance artists," Hughes wrote. She was "full of side-splitting anecdotes, humorous tales, and tragicomic stories."

Hurston also could be unorthodox. One day for subway fare she borrowed a nickel from a blind beggar's cup. She told him she would repay him, but that today she needed the fare more than him. Hurston had fun shocking people with her lack of regard for conventional behavior. At the time it was scandalous for women to be seen smoking in public. Hurston however enjoyed waltzing down the street, cigarette in hand.

Hurston had no fear of being alone on the streets. Her tough life had prepared her well. One evening, on her way to a party, a man made a pass at her as she stood in an elevator. Despite her long white dress and wide hat, she threw a right punch, then stepped out of the elevator without a glance at the flattened man on the floor behind her.

Hurston's new life thrilled her. This spirit, this joy gave Hurston her first chances for true self expression. "I am just running wild in every direction, trying to see everything at once," Hurston wrote to Herbert Sheen's sister Constance.

In June of 1926 Hurston moved into her own apartment, despite having no furniture. She furnished it by having a party. Everyone who came brought a piece of furniture or a decoration, in exchange for some of Hurston's cooking.

She called it a hand-chicken dinner; everyone ate with their hands as Hurston had no forks. Within a few days Hurston had a furnished apartment with everything from decorative silver birds to a footstool in her living room. Her apartment soon became a popular spot. She kept a pot on the stove and visitors often brought something to contribute to the pot, creating a common stew. Other times Hurston enjoyed treating guests to her specialties: fried shrimp, fried okra, gingerbread, cooked Florida eels, or a jug of cool buttermilk. Hurston's apartment was always open for someone to stay, and sometimes she spent hours consoling a depressed fellow artist. Sometimes when having a party at her apartment, she wanted to work. She retreated to her bedroom and asked for the last person out to lock the door.

Hurston also sometimes paid her rent in the popular fashion of having a rent party. Everyone paid a dime or a quarter to attend the party, often held on a Thursday or Sunday night, when many of the attendees who worked as maids were off work. This helped the host to pay the rent, which in Harlem was $20.00 to $30.00 higher than rent in other parts of the city. Segregated housing practices didn't give black people the option of leaving Harlem and moving to cheaper neighborhoods. African Americans spent more than 40 percent of their income on rent. Sometimes at these rent parties professional musicians, such as Fats Waller and Duke Ellington showed up after a paying gig. Their music often set off frenzied dancing of the Charleston. The menu typically featured cuisine of black southerners: rice, black-eye peas, collard greens, potato salad, and chicken.

Hurston was perfectly placed in Harlem. In 1918 a con-stitutional amendment had been passed banning alcoholic

The Cotton Club operated as a popular Harlem speakeasy during the Prohibition era. *(Courtesy of Frank Driggs Collection/Getty Images)*

beverages. While buying and selling alcohol was illegal, even the most dedicated churchgoers had contacts with bootleggers who sold alcohol. Gangsters and bootleggers paid off policemen, and opened clubs called speakeasies where people drank liquor. Speakeasies with colorful names such as Basement Brownies Coal Bin, The Clam House, and The Cotton Club spread throughout Harlem, Times Square, and New York's financial district. But Harlem was the center of it all. In a speakeasy people could drink, dance, and gamble. Prohibition wouldn't end until 1933.

In 1920, Hurston and the rest of the country were caught up in the Roaring Twenties, also called the Lawless Decade, the Flapper Era, the Dollar Decade, and the Jazz Age. After the horrors of World War I, the United States launched into an era of revelry, rebellion, prosperity, and modernization. During the war, the government had monitored the railroads, coal supplies, and gasoline consumption. They urged people to observe meatless Mondays and wheatless Wednesdays to provide more for the soldiers overseas. Now people wanted more freedom and to be able to enjoy life. They launched one of the most carefree periods of American life.

Attitudes and opportunities changed as people sought those freedoms. Women got the right to vote in 1920 and more and more of them took jobs outside of the home. With their new independence, women also began to dress differently, wearing chin-length hair, sheer silk stockings, and short dresses, and they loved to shock others by smoking, chewing gum, and using slang, such as baloney (nonsense) and the cat's meow (wonderful).

A new kind of music symbolized the freedom of the era. Originating in New Orleans, jazz was exciting and energetic. The music came of age in black nightclubs and dance halls around the country. Musical greats such as Louis Armstrong, Fats Waller, and Duke Ellington had thrilled African American crowds for years. Then in 1921 the black musical *Shuffle Along* crashed onto the scene. It was the first performance in years by a black troupe on Broadway, and white Americans were swept up by these catchy rhythms.

Conservative Americans judged jazz as being primitive and barbaric because of its African American roots. Some even attributed its evil influence to the country's decline in moral values. But younger generations loved the music. It represented a tempting forbidden fruit and they were thrilled by the idea that they were smashing taboos. One of the most famous songs of the time was "Shake that Thing" by Ethel Waters. It was an age of flappers in whirling fringed dresses, fast moving Charleston feet, and alcohol-filled hip flasks.

A group of flappers participating in a Charleston dance contest in 1926 *(Courtesy of Hulton Archive/Getty Images)*

Harlem and the Jazz Age had its own slang. As a writer and lover of language, Hurston savored the feelings and the sounds of the words. She soaked up the spirit of the age as she attended parties and listened to people talk about "Russians" meaning southern blacks who had rushed up North and "conkbusters," meaning either cheap liquors or intellectual African Americans.

Hurston loved Harlem. For her the city held possibilities, especially "when I set my hat at a certain angle and saunter down Seventh Avenue, Harlem City, feeling as snooty as the lions in front of the Forty-Second St. Library," she said.

Many people in the 1920s became fascinated with black life and culture. White writers went out of their way to meet African Americans at parties. They invited them to other events and asked them to serve as their passport to Harlem. Sometimes African Americans rubbed elbows with their white patrons at their evening parties only to wait unrecognized for a tip the next day when carrying their hostess's bags during their day jobs as redcaps, or hotel workers.

This craze and interest in black culture originated in the theater with black revues or shows. African American art, literature, music, and dance soared in popularity.

"Caucasians stormed Harlem," commented writer Rudolph Fisher. Nights in Harlem clubs represented excursions into exotic territories.

Novelist Fannie Hurst was no different. She once took Hurston on a trip to Vermont and passed her off as an African princess to forcibly integrate a local restaurant. While Hurst considered it a victory, Hurston knew that the stunt had accomplished little. "Who would think that a good meal could be so bitter," she commented.

Carl Van Vechten *(Library of Congress)*

For Hurston, straddling Barnard's white world of tennis, golf, and riding lessons and her rich folk community of Harlem, complete with rent parties, was difficult.

Another man interested in black culture was novelist and critic Carl Van Vechten. He frequently gave interracial parties, and became widely known as "a sincere friend of the Negro."

Alain Locke *(Courtesy of Yale Collection of American Literature, Beinecke Rare Book and Manuscript Library)*

Hurston was a frequent guest at his parties, a sign among Harlem artists that she had arrived and made her mark. Her white friends included stockbrokers, journalists, publishing executives, artists, and editors. Hurston and other artists were left constantly trying to decipher the sincerity of such sudden white interest in their culture and work.

Hurston and her fellow artists followed their love of writing, but soon they began to feel outside pressures shaping their work. Hurston's professor at Howard, Alain Locke, edited a magazine called *The New Negro*. Locke was a Rhodes scholar, a Harvard graduate, and a philosophy professor. In his magazine he displayed the creative works of Hurston, Langston Hughes, and others to further racial relations.

Locke had published Hurston's story "Spunk." The story rested on supernatural beliefs characteristic to black folklife. Set in an Eatonville-type village, a man named Spunk steals someone's wife then shoots him. The man's ghost haunts Spunk, first as a black cat, then as an invisible force that pushes him into suicide. Locke wanted his artists' work to be both beautiful and propagandistic so that whites realized black talent. Often for him this meant what Hurston called mimicking white writers. Instead she envisioned creating art that reflected and spoke to the community and the common element, such as folklore. To Hurston, Locke acted like a mother hen, trying to cluck at her and keep his flock in line. He sometimes disapproved of her work and her lack of discipline. Although Locke respected her talent, he didn't hesitate to give her advice. He relied on Hurston and others to interpret race for the world. It was a heavy burden with which Hurston and the others were uncomfortable. "Youth speaks, and the voice of the 'New Negro' is heard," Locke said.

Hurston increasingly chafed under Locke's control and attitudes. She simply wanted to write and to tell stories, and she did not want to use her writings as a political soapbox from which to preach her ideas. She commented she was sick of the race problem and just wanted to write a novel, not a sociology book. Eventually Hurston tired of Locke, saying he was, "a malicious, spiteful little snot that thinks he ought to be the leading Negro because of his degrees."

It was difficult to not get involved though. Black people were still being lynched, and the United States government still hadn't passed an anti-lynching bill. Fiery statements charged the atmosphere. "The American Negro demands equality—political equality, industrial equality, and social equality; and he is never going to rest until satisfied with anything less," said W. E. B. Du Bois.

Intensely private with her personal life, Hurston did not use her life experiences to expound on racism, unlike other black authors such as Richard Wright. Wright had grown up in the rural south, left home at an early age, and had worked in a series of low paying jobs. He had bitter memories of these years, and believed that all black authors had a political and emotional duty to describe the horrors of racism. Both Hurston and Wright were brilliant writers, but with powerfully different visions of black life.

"I am not tragically colored. There is not great sorrow dammed up in my soul, nor lurking behind my eyes . . . ," Hurston said. "I do not belong to the sobbing school of Negrohood who hold that nature somehow has given them a lowdown dirty deal," she wrote in May of 1928 for an article in the magazine *World Tomorrow*. Her hometown, her family, and her independence had all helped to build her strong self confidence.

In the summer of 1926 Hurston and her fellow artists decided to launch their own magazine. They called it *Fire!!* The magazine was purely artistic, unlike other magazines where their talents were used for ending racism. The artists enjoyed shocking stuffy people. They met frequently to discuss literature and politics. They also gossiped and partied late into the evening. The artists decided *Fire!!* would be

Richard Wright *(Library of Congress)*

paid for and published solely by themselves, which would prove to be no small feat. One of Hurston's comrades was Wallace Thurman, a novelist and loyal friend. Torn by never creating art that lived up to his standards, Thurman's sarcastic humor led him to be a gifted critic of the times. Another comrade was Langston Hughes, a quiet observer of the scene, who was well on his way to becoming Harlem's poet laureate, acclaimed for his artistic poetic ability.

Langston Hughes *(Library of Congress)*

When telling Locke about the new magazine, Hurston explained there needed to be "more outlets for Negro fire." For the magazine's first issue Hurston reworked her story "Color Struck." She also wrote a story titled "Sweat." In it Hurston tells the tale of a washerwoman and her unemployed husband. Her labor supports them, but his insecurities lead to a love/hate relationship.

From the beginning problems plagued *Fire!!* The six contributing artists each agreed to put in fifty dollars toward production. Only three did though, as no one had much money. Editing continued slowly. Hurston continued to study at Barnard. Hughes returned to college in Pennsylvania. Other projects occupied the artists, and the magazine was short of both material and funds. Thurman headed the editorial board and took on debts of nearly one thousand dollars. Everyone tried to help as much as they could. Finally several hundred copies were printed, but burned in the basement of an apartment house. Hurston quipped that although *Fire!!* had gone to ashes, the idea was still a good one.

When the magazine finally came out, its first and only issue, some critics panned it. Overall the artists strived to get the magazine banned somewhere by shocking and encouraging new types of artistic energy and interest. *Fire!!* went out of its way to challenge Victorian moralities with stories of prostitution and homosexuality. Some critics however call it Hurston's best fiction of the period.

While continuing her writing, Hurston had developed a new interest at Barnard—the world of anthropology, or study of human societies. She learned under the direction of Franz Boas, a German émigré, who had founded the first anthropology department in the United States in 1899. Now Hurston followed his direction and began to do field work. For Hurston, who hated routine, anthropology was different from the regular grind. At a time when many anthropologists believed that nonwhite peoples were primitive, Boas argued differently, believing no race to be superior. To prove his point Hurston stood on the corner of Harlem streets measuring people's skulls to disprove the claim that African Americans

Franz Boas on the cover of *Time* magazine *(Courtesy of R. H. Hoffmann/Time Magazine/Time & Life Pictures/Getty Image)*

had smaller heads, and therefore smaller brains, so were less intelligent. This study of human body measurement was so outrageous that it suited Hurston perfectly.

"Almost nobody else could stop the average Harlemite . . . and measure his head with a strange-looking anthropological device and not get bawled out in the attempt, except Zora, who used to stop anyone whose head looked interesting, and measure it," said Hughes.

Anthropology gave Hurston a new lens through which to view people. So far her personal success as a writer had revolved around her storytelling, usually about an Eatonville-type environment. She had represented a known but largely unexplored segment of American black life, adding to the Harlem Renaissance as few others could with her tales of the rural south. Now her Barnard education allowed her to step back and analyze her experiences. Folktales no longer were simple stories. The humor and superstitions within each tale represented a priceless contribution to her own cultural anthropology. The stories were among the most vital parts of her life and the impetus for her imagination. Boas encouraged Hurston to study African American culture and to record African American folklore. He helped her receive funding for her first such study.

Hurston had entered New York City in early 1925 as a writer. Now two years later her education at Barnard had shaped her into a serious social scientist as well. Her studies with Franz Boas gave her a new fascination with which to tackle the world. She had added another layer to the writer within her and set out to combine her talents with her rich background and love of African American folklore.

Hurston poses with dolls during her time studying anthropology under Franz Boas. *(Courtesy of the Stetson Kennedy Foundation Collection, Zora Neale Hurston Collection, George A. Smathers Libraries, University of Florida, Department of Special Collections)*

four

Traveling Dust

In February of 1927 Hurston hopped on a train to central Florida. She planned to collect folklore for six months by recording some of the customs, songs, tales, superstitions, lies, jokes, dances, and games that made up African American folklore. Her travels were funded by a $1,400 fellowship from Columbia University's anthropology department. She was working for Franz Boas and Carter Woodson of the Association for the Study of Negro Life and History. The idea of collecting such lore was in its early stages of infancy, and was especially treasured by black collectors. It was an untapped field and Hurston already had an intimate knowledge of the south. After traveling to Jacksonville, Florida she would move west to Mobile, Alabama.

Folklore can be stories or sayings passed from generation to generation, such as the tall tales of Paul Bunyan the lumberjack or the superstition that breaking a mirror leads to seven years of bad luck. There are also folksongs, such as "Swing Low, Sweet Chariot," that tell of feelings or events of a particular culture or time. There is also folk art, such as the hex signs on the barns of Pennsylvania Dutch farmers, and folk dances, such as the square dances of Texas ranchers.

"In folklore as in all other forms of human behavior, the world is a great big old serving platter and all the localities are like eating plates," Hurston once said. "All of the plates get helped with food from the platter, but each plate seasons to suit itself . . . that is what is known as originality."

On Hurston's way south she had stopped in Memphis for a reunion with her brothers. Bob now apologized for not helping her more with school, like he had promised years earlier. Hurston also saw her brother Benjamin, now a pharmacist

A strip of film negatives taken during a folklore-collecting trip to Belle Glade, Florida. Hurston appears in negatives nine and eleven. *(Library of Congress)*

working in Memphis. She caught up on the actions of the rest of the family. Clifford Joel was a high school principal in Alabama. Richard worked as a traveling chef on the East Coast. Sarah lived the life of a preacher's wife and mother. John Cornelius worked at a market in Jacksonville. Everett was a postal worker in Brooklyn. The family had gone in different directions and spread out across the country. However, Hurston had some closure with her family since the loss of their mother, Lucy.

Along the way in her travels Hurston bought an old car that she nicknamed Sassie Susie. The South proved challenging for African American travelers. Often Hurston pulled Sassie Susie over to the high roadside grasses to go to the bathroom as "whites only" signs blocked other options. After long hours of traveling by herself she was forced to search towns for black neighborhoods where she could find lodging and food.

Hurston turned her attention to her job at hand. Folklore to her was an art form that people create before they learn that there is such a thing as art. It comes from folks wondering about natural laws and nature. She believed that these interpretations, which some may call crude or unscientific, often are wise and poetic explanations for the ways of the world.

For Hurston the blues, folktales, and spirituals were a special code of communication. Instead of merely emulating white culture, this authentic folklore emphasized the diversity and beauty of African American culture.

The first generation of freed slaves after the American Civil War had often repudiated their folk heritage as a product of slavery. Their music and poems of suffering, called sorrow songs, and even their dialect became taboo as incorrect English.

Hurston wears a pistol and stands in front of Sassie Susie during one of her folklore-collecting trips. *(Courtesy of the Stetson Kennedy Foundation Collection, Zora Neale Hurston Collection, George A. Smathers Libraries, University of Florida, Department of Special Collections)*

But Hurston embraced this heritage, believing it to be just as valid as classical music, as it expressed beautiful emotion. She brought this feeling to the Harlem Renaissance.

But Hurston's attention wasn't entirely on collecting folklore. Herbert Sheen had traveled to Florida from Chicago's Rush Medical College. Their relationship had lasted throughout her years at Howard and Barnard and their separation. On May 19, 1927, while she was in St. Augustine, Florida, she finally married Sheen. On the eve of their wedding Hurston had a dream about the problems in both her mother's and sister's marriages. She feared that marrying Sheen would only narrow her life. Were they marrying out of love or a sense of comfort and familiarity? Regardless, they married and as Hurston worked the newlyweds traveled together.

The morning after their wedding, aviator Charles Lindbergh took off from New York for the first successful nonstop flight across the Atlantic Ocean. He landed triumphantly in Paris on May 21. The world celebrated his victory, but for Hurston deep in the South, she was already having more misgivings about her marriage.

Sheen "could stomp a piano out of this world, sing a fair baritone, and dance beautifully," Hurston wrote. "For the first time since my mother's death there was someone who felt really close and warm to me." However they were at odds. Both had promising careers that they didn't want to give up. When Sheen returned to Chicago, Hurston stayed in the South continuing her own work.

As Hurston rambled through small towns, she realized that collecting folklore was more difficult that she had imagined. Since leaving Eatonville, Hurston had changed.

"The glamour of Barnard College was still upon me. I dwelt in marble halls. I knew where the material was all right. But I went about asking in carefully accented Barnardese, 'Pardon me, but do you know any folktales or folksongs?'"

By May Hurston still had little to report. She knew she should collect songs, classify them, compare them, and determine their significance to African American culture. Yet Hurston had trouble with the scientific discipline required to collect folklore.

She was playing many roles: a member of the Eatonville folk community, a Barnard student fascinated with western civilization, and anthropologist/folklorist documenting African American culture, a creative writer contributing to literary traditions, and to some a New Negro seeking to repudiate racial stereotypes. Hurston struggled to bridge all of these gaps.

On Hurston's way through Mobile, Alabama she met up with Langston Hughes. She confided to him about her recent marriage, a fact she had concealed from Franz Boas as he would think she wasn't serious in pursuing her work. She worried that Boas might resent her as just another woman scholar who got married and abandoned her work. Now over fried fish and watermelon they decided to drive north together in Sassie Susie. The good friends laughed and joked, picking up folk songs and tall tales along the way. Hughes could not drive, but Hurston welcomed his company. She happily wrote to their friend Carl Van Vechten, "We are charging home in a wheezy car and hope to be home for Xmas. We are being fed on watermelon, chicken, and the company of good things. Wish you were with us."

Hurston returned to New York and contributed a story to the *Journal of Negro History* in October 1927. She wrote about Cudjo Lewis, the only survivor of the last known slave ship to the United States. At eighty years old he vividly remembered Africa and its cultural differences. In short, he was a treasure trove of information and a major scientific resource. But Hurston's report only contained about 25 percent research; the rest was plagiarized. She never acknowledged Emma Langdon Roche's book that had used Lewis as a source. It will never be known why she took such a huge academic risk. By using someone else's work without citing it, she jeopardized her entire professional career. Perhaps she had little success interviewing Lewis, maybe he had a heavy accent, or she didn't ask the right questions. Maybe she was realizing the tiresome difficulty of collecting folklore or feeling the effects of a disintegrating marriage. Possibly Hurston was torn between writing creatively and reporting as a scientist. Either way, luckily for her, Hurston's plagiarism wasn't discovered until 1972. She spent the next few months organizing the material she had collected. Franz Boas expressed his disappointment, but it was not as bad as Hurston had expected.

In mid-September 1927 Hurston received an invitation to visit Charlotte Osgood Mason, Langston Hughes's patron. An elderly white woman, Mason was a generous patron of the African American arts. A friend of presidents, this elegant woman had spent months living amongst a tribe of Plains Indians working on a project about American Indians. Over the years she anonymously contributed between fifty to 75,000 dollars to African American artists, or nearly $750,000 today.

Charlotte Osgood Mason *(Courtesy of Yale Collection of American Literature, Beinecke Rare Book and Manuscript Library)*

When Hurston first entered Mason's house she was reminded of one of her childhood visions. Hurston had dreamed of two women, one old and one young. One of the women had been arranging strangely shaped flowers, which Hurston now realized were calla lilies. In her vision she had sensed that when she came to these women it would be the "end of my pilgrimage but not the end of my life."

Hurston and Mason found common interests in that they both believed in the simple and natural honesty of folklore. This mutual feeling forged a relationship that would benefit Hurston over the next several years. Hurston enjoyed Mason and found her fascinating.

She once said of Mason, "There she was sitting up there at the table over capon, caviar, and gleaming silver, eager to hear every word on every phase of life on a sawmill job. I must tell the tales, sing the songs, do the dances, and report the raucous sayings and doings of the Negro farthest down."

Mason agreed to fund another one of Hurston's folklore collecting trips. This contract would last from the beginning of 1928 through December of 1930. Hurston would put together a collection of folklore that would become Mason's property, as she didn't trust that Hurston would know best what to do with it. Mason demanded that Hurston collect, but not publish anything without her approval. Mason was very controlling of her protégés, her money giving her leverage.

Mason "possessed the power to control people's lives—pick them up and put them down when and where she wished," Hughes once commented.

Yet Mason had laid the groundwork to establish Hurston as a famed folklorist. Over the next five years she would donate nearly $15,000 to Hurston. Hurston's dependence on her patron often led to bitterness, yet she called Mason her "Godmother."

Although Hurston chafed under Mason's commands and complained that she was walking a tightrope, she had a budget of two hundred dollars a month, a car, a boss who would be one thousand miles away, and a new folklore excursion.

Before Hurston set off on her latest trip, she and Sheen abandoned their marriage. Hurston's relationship with her husband had continued to be a long-distance one. She had kept her own last name, an action that was unheard of at the time. Few knew the couple had even married.

"I hear that my husband has divorced me, so that's that," Hurston wrote to a friend. "Don't think I am upset . . . He was one of the obstacles that worried me."

Hurston and her former husband remained friends but she was focused and driven to succeed, just as she had always been. Sheen himself pointed out that they were each full of their own work. The couple did not divorce each other until July 7, 1931, waiting until they could afford the legal paperwork.

Again Hurston hopped in her car and headed home to Eatonville. She moved in with a friend and invited people to visit. During these visits Hurston plied her guests with buttermilk and gingerbread in exchange for stories, tales, songs, and lies. Hurston also was invited to one of Eatonville's social traditions—a "toe party." During the party all of the women stood behind a sheet with only their toes sticking out. After looking at the toes, each gentleman bought a toe for a dime. Then he treated the toe's owner to refreshments and dancing. Hurston's toe was bought five times, but after five servings of fried chicken she either had to "get another stomach or quit eating," she recalled.

Next Hurston headed to Polk County, Florida, an area filled with lumber camps. These camps formed communities of laborers and their families, who worked hard during the day and played hard at night, especially on payday. After dark they went to the jook joints or bars where "pay night rocks on with music and gambling and laughter and dancing and fights," Hurston said. It was a rough and tumble world, but also one filled with folktales, sayings, songs, and jokes. Even confident Hurston was "timid as an egg without a shell"

A jook joint at a Florida labor camp *(Library of Congress)*

in the jook joints, she admitted. She needed protection and found it in a large, knife-wielding woman named Big Sweet. Both the black workers and white bosses respected Big Sweet. She helped Hurston find good storytellers and lying contests. It was some of the most concentrated collecting of Hurston's career.

At the first lying session Hurston promised four prizes to the biggest and best lies. The results thrilled her. Each person tried to top the previous teller's tale. Mosquitoes were a favorite topic. Two men, Will House and Joe Wiley, told about a mosquito that ate an entire cow and was luring the calf to the same fate. Another man, nicknamed Black Baby, commented that that was just a baby mosquito. Ones he knew sang like male alligators and could screw on longer bills so they could bite and draw blood through four thick blankets. The tales went on and on, and Hurston recorded them all excitedly.

The "most gorgeous possibilities are showing themselves constantly," she said. They were also giving her ideas for opera scenes, about which she wrote to Hughes.

One night Hurston decided to go to the jook joint alone. She joined the men to collect stories in a woofing, or casual talking, session. One of women didn't like Hurston's sweet talking the men and drew a knife on her, blocking the joint's only door. Fortunately Big Sweet appeared. While knives flashed, razors slashed, and even ice picks cut the air, Hurston dashed out the door to her car, barely escaping.

Hurston decided to collect her tales during the daytime for her own safety. She and some of the sawmill workers planned a fishing trip. With their homemade lines they walked two miles under mossy trees to the lake. Out on the water, while catching fat trout and slapping away at mosquitoes, Hurston heard tales about how 'gator lost his tongue and why mockingbirds don't fly on Fridays.

Hurston longed to publish the colorful tales instantly, but Mason had demanded that she only collect. Conflict arose when Hurston's essay "How It Feels to Be Colored Me" appeared in the magazine *World Tomorrow* in May 1928. Although Hurston had submitted the essay months earlier, Mason was outraged, feeling Hurston had broken their contract. Hurston's old professor Alain Locke helped mediate the situation.

By now Hurston knew she was on to something significant for the literary and anthropological world. She began to organize her collections in her mind, all the while writing conspiratorial letters to Hughes about her work. For now she bided her time and continued working.

Next she moved on to New Orleans. The question of African American religious beliefs had begun to fascinate her. Hurston planned to delve into the world of voudou. Depending on the decade and the area, the religion has been called many different names. In the American South it has been called hoodoo, voodoo, or voudou, the original Creole-based spelling. It is called vodun in Haiti, santeria in Cuba, curanderismo in Mexico, and obeah in Jamaica. Today some estimate that there are nearly 50 million adherents worldwide.

The religion originated in the ancient West African kingdom of Yoruba, roughly the area of Nigeria today. There, the African spirits were called the *orisha* and in the neighboring country of Benin, the *vo-du*. From 1440 to 1880, slave ships delivered about 12 million Africans, mainly captured from the western coast of Africa, to Caribbean and Atlantic

A man participating in a voudou ceremony in which the goddess Mami Wata is called upon to help free him from sorcery. *(Courtesy of Black Star/Alamy)*

ports. The captured slaves represented a variety of regions, cities, and languages. Although they brought their cultural and religious beliefs with them, these were quickly outlawed and only Christian worship was allowed. Unable to openly practice their beliefs, slaves devised methods of combining or linking gods. Slaves might pray to St. Barbara, while really praying to the vo-du thunder god, Songo. The African god's red and white colors and favorite weapon, the double-headed axe, matched St. Barbara's.

In these ways, voudou changed. Although it still had an African core, it mixed with other faiths and beliefs from Brazil to New Orleans. It borrowed from native Indians, European witchcraft, and even other African customs. It also adopted elements of Catholicism to outwardly appear Christian. Today, voudou refers to any of the religious practices in the New World that originated with the Yoruba religion and kingdom, even though in different areas it has different names, rituals, and practices.

To some, voudou was merely magic, but to others it was a complex religion filled with ancient traditions. Based on the belief that there are magic and supernatural forces swirling around us, voudou invokes chants, prayers, songs, dances, and ritual sacrifices of animals such as sheep, goats, and chickens.

Voudou doctors, also called root workers, or conjurers, could remedy a situation with magical powers or folk remedies. Many southern black people in the 1920s and 1930s had little faith in medicine, instead turning to the folk remedies of their ancestors. They might see a root doctor to cure anything from blindness to skin problems. These doctors could heal illnesses, especially if an enemy was responsible, by placing a hex on the foe. They also could resolve tangled love affairs. In extreme cases they could harm or kill a person's enemies. To voudou followers, the word mojo meant a magical charm that warded off hexes.

One example of a doctor's work was to break up a love affair by taking nine needles and breaking them up into three pieces each. Talismans, or lucky charms, also played roles. A shell wrapped in human hair would bring about love. Voudou dolls, candles, and pictures could be used either to harm or to worship a person.

Hurston now planned to completely immerse herself in the lives of people who practiced these beliefs. Amidst the cathedrals, speakeasies, and brothels of New Orleans, there was an underlying element of voudou believers. Practicing voudou was against the law in New Orleans, so believers secretly passed their knowledge through a powerful silent grapevine that bound them together. Hurston had to secretly find the conjurers and convince them that she meant no harm, but was sincerely interested. She sought out the grandnephew of Marie Leveau, a legendary Creole conjurer. Leveau was descended from three generations of voudou queens. Her spirit presided over the meeting, along with a huge rattlesnake. Leveau's grandnephew was wrapped in his great aunt's snakeskin.

Over the months Hurston spent collecting voudou folklore, she underwent initiation rituals and psychic experiences. She had lightning symbols painted across her back and drank blood mixed with wine. In another ceremony she bathed in a warm bath of salt, sugar, perfume, and parsley water as two long pink candles burned. Then she was told what spirits to ask for favors. Hurston also became a Boss of the Candles, meaning one who works with spirits, after she participated in a ritual called the Pea Vine Candle Drill. Using a black candle, she lit eight blue candles and set them in front of an altar to form the shape of a serpent.

Hurston was not just collecting the techniques but often reporting them as being successful. Many have questioned whether she herself believed in the principles and powers of voudou. All we know is that she said while exploring the rituals in the moonlit dampness of swamps she found voudou both "beautiful and terrifying." In one of her books she wrote about whether she believed, "I don't know . . . always I have to say the same thing. I don't know. I don't know."

From August 1928 to the end of the year Hurston had made the transition from an artist interested in folklore to a thoughtful scholar. She retreated to a small cabin in the coastal village of Eau Gallie, near St. Augustine, Florida and organized her notes. Hurston planned to write about the universality of human beliefs. From Eatonville, Florida to New York City Hurston wanted to show that all civilizations have ties to each other. She struggled to find the best genre to present her folklore and to bring it to life. Hurston could write well enough to do it, but she worried about breathing life into the songs and dances. By May of 1929 she had finished her first draft of the folktale collections, entitling it *Mules and Men*.

Hurston set the book aside to cool for a while. She wanted time to give herself time to let the manuscript develop inside her mind. Only a month later though Hurston grew seriously ill with liver problems. She had been plagued with such problems for the last two years. After a hospital stay, she slowly began to recover. Ever dedicated to her quest, by

August 29 while in Miami, Hurston finished the second and third drafts of *Mules and Men* and sent the manuscript to Mason in New York.

Hurston was not free to leave Mason's employment yet though. Mason still held a legal hold over Hurston's work. *Mules and Men* sat in Godmother's safe deposit box in New York, representing two years of Hurston's work. Unfortunately, deeper forces were also swirling around Hurston. She and the rest of the country stood poised to take a deep emotional and financial plunge.

From 1920 to 1930, the country had been on a spending spree. Gradually, the number of factories had increased. Stock market prices had steadily increased from the end of World War I in 1919. In 1924 stock averaged $120 a share. Five years later the average had increased to more than four hundred dollars. People made millions of dollars on the stock market. Famed millionaire, Jacob Raskob, quipped, "Not only can one be rich, but one ought to be rich."

People had money to spare, and they spent it on fads. They bought radios and listened to radio shows. They consulted Ouija Boards and played Mah-Jong, a Chinese game that is a kind of combination of dice and dominoes. Adults smoked cigarettes, while children gobbled up candy from Pez dispensers. People bought brand new Model-T cars. Also in the 1920s they flocked to theaters to see "talkies," the first movies that had sound.

With so many new products on the market, combined with the increase in factories, the markets were flooded with items to buy. Slick advertising encouraged people to play a role in the country's prosperity. But wealth in the United States was poorly distributed. Most people were either wealthy or poor. America housed 27.5 million families, and 21.5 million of them made three thousand dollars a year, about $33,000 today. These families could ill afford to buy extra goods. But they bought cars, clothes, houses, furniture, radios, and much more, on credit that they couldn't afford.

The more everyone bought, the higher the stock market rose. Stock represents the value of the company, and in the 1920s stocks increased more than many companies were actually worth. It was a rumbling economic earthquake. As more people bought items on credit, businesses began to struggle. Factories couldn't afford to continue to make their products or to pay their employees.

Insiders, or people who had inside information about a company's finances, began to sell their shares quickly, as they knew of the companies' difficulties. On October 24, 1929, a day which would become known as Black Tuesday, this stock market roller coaster crashed from its highest peak to its lowest valley. Stock prices plummeted by the hour. Everyone tried to sell their shares of stock in the companies, but no one wanted to buy a portion of a doomed company. Panicked, confused people rushed through the streets. The vast heap of ruined companies mounted, setting off a vicious cycle. The banks that had loaned the companies money also went under. Workers lost their jobs and couldn't pay their bills. Businesses failed because no one could afford to buy their goods or to make their payments. Within a year, the country's average income had dropped from $847 to $465, and more than 9 million workers in the United States were unemployed.

The Great Depression swept like a plague over the country. It affected the rich and the poor. Men, women, and children,

A panicked crowd in the Wall Street district of Manhattan during the stock market crash of 1929 (*Courtesy of AP Images*)

whether they were black or white, native or foreign born, urban workers or farmers—all reeled from the economic impact of the stock market's crash. Millions of people lost their jobs, their businesses, their farms, their homes, their savings, and ultimately their self respect as few could provide for themselves or their families.

Each family dealt with the Great Depression differently. Some parents tried to pretend nothing was wrong so as not to worry their children. People couldn't afford medical care when their family members grew sick, and lived without heat or adequate food. There was no shame in substituting a grain sack for a sweater or stuffing cardboard into shoes

Men standing in a bread line during the Great Depression *(Library of Congress)*

to cover holes. People lived from meal to meal. City govern-
ments, churches, and charities distributed as much food as
they could. Breadlines in New York City served two thousand
people a day. Hungry mobs in Chicago ransacked garbage
dumps throughout the city on a daily basis.

During the Depression childhood ended early for kids.
Hundreds of thousands of families were evicted from their
homes and farms. They lived in tents and shacks made of
cardboard, scrap wood, and metal. More than 1 million children had stopped receiving educations because there was
no money to pay teachers. Many children and their families
became migrant workers, traveling between fields to earn

money for food. Other children worked in factories for ten hours a day to help make ends meet. Such factory jobs were prized.

The country had sunk into an economic and emotional depression. Music of the time ranged from somber songs reflecting the country's mood to silly tunes attempting to make people forget their doldrums. Lyrics such as "Jeepers, creepers, where'd you get those peepers," tried to bring a smile. Cheap entertainment abounded. Swing and Jitterbug contests grew popular as people jumped, hopped, stomped, and bounced their cares away for an hour or two. People frequented public libraries because of their free circulation. Stories such as Pearl S. Buck's *The Good Earth* about Chinese peasants and Margaret Mitchell's *Gone With the Wind* about a fiery Southern belle appealed to people who wanted triumphant stories in the face of a bleak world. A new fad, chain letters, also spread across the country, as people wished, hoped, and prayed for good luck.

Even before the Depression hit, unemployment was higher in black communities. Because discrimination was widespread across the United States, many businesses refused to hire black workers. This grim reality only worsened once the stock market crashed. From the Civil War until 1929 many white Americans considered it demeaning to work as a janitor, barber, elevator operator, street cleaner, garbage collector, maid, cook, shoe shiner, or porter on a train. African Americans typically found work in such service areas, or in steel mills, slaughterhouses, or as cowboys or entertainers. But when the Depression hit, white workers eagerly pounced on these jobs. Rumors of any job often attracted hundreds or even thousands of applicants. With so many people seeking jobs, black workers were often completely shut out. During the Depression 56 percent of the black community was out of work compared to 39 percent of the white community. Hurston was no different, but being short of money was nothing new to her. She continued to search for more tales to tell.

Around Christmas of 1929 Hurston traveled to the Bahamas to collect more folklore. She learned more about conjuring spirits, and stayed for carnival. Revelers paraded through the streets in colorful costumes, beating goatskin drums, clanging cowbells, and tweeting whistles. One of the worst hurricanes in years hit the islands. For five days 150-mph winds whipped the islands mercilessly. On the second night, as the storm raged, Hurston, who was living with a family, had a premonition. She leaped from her bed and urged everyone out of the house, which collapsed moments later. Hurston feared she would never get back to the mainland, but eventually the storm abated.

In January or early February of 1930 Hurston sailed home to New York with only her return ticket and twenty-four cents to her name. By now she had collected nearly 95,000 words of stories, songs, children's games, conjuring and related material, and photos. She planned to organize and compile them into a book. She contacted her former teacher Boas and sought his advice with her material. He cautioned her, saying some of her voudou material may be contentious, but Hurston was never one to be dissuaded. By contacting Boas she was directly defying Godmother's stringent requirements. Hurston never was quite one for rules.

After Hurston returned north she took up residence in a boardinghouse in Westfield, New Jersey, about twenty miles outside of New York City. She now had help sorting out

Louise Thompson *(Courtesy of Yale Collection of American Literature, Beinecke Rare Book and Manuscript Library)*

her material. Louise Thompson, a young literary secretary employed by Mason, worked for both Hurston and Hughes. Often Thompson typed halfway through the night to prepare Hurston's manuscript. Hurston's material was so extensive that this process took two years.

While Hurston prepared her manuscript she also was engaged in a complex emotional struggle with Mason. Her old professor Locke again helped mediate the friction between the two women. Hurston's faithful friend, Langston Hughes, advised her on the politics of her situation and on Mason's feelings about her. He suggested Hurston write frequently and send Mason items such as wood carvings, orange blossoms, and melons from her collecting trips. Matters boiled down to the simple fact that Hurston needed Mason's financial support, despite any strings that came attached to it. Hurston was faced with stacks and stacks of field notes that needed to be condensed and organized. The bottom line was that Mason controlled all of this material.

For a diversion from her folklore cataloging, Hurston turned her attention to an idea that had long been simmering. For years she and Hughes had discussed staging an African American opera. They wanted to write a real comedy, not just a minstrel show. They had excitedly traded ideas back and forth. While Hurston was collecting folklore in Florida she had proposed to Hughes that they call the opera "Jook" after the bars at saw mills and turpentine stills. Now Mason supported the idea as well. Hurston and Hughes worked on the opera from May through June of 1930.

The opera began as a tale of two hunters who both shoot and kill a wild turkey. They argue over who killed it until one knocks the other unconscious with a bone from a mule. With help from Thompson, Hurston and Hughes collaborated. Hurston proposed skits, songs, and music that blended African American and African Caribbean culture and folklore. In four weeks time they had drafts of the first and third act and one scene of the second.

In June Hurston traveled to Florida, taking the second act with her to complete. This was the beginning of a falling out

Hurston stands with Hughes in 1927. *(Courtesy of Yale Collection of American Literature, Beinecke Rare Book and Manuscript Library)*

between the two friends. Though the opera seemed to be progressing smoothly, Hurston left because she was angry about Hughes's friendship with Thompson. He had suggested they make Thompson their business manager, and Hurston was furious. She and Hughes had talked about collaborating for years. To Hurston, Thompson was a third wheel. According to Hughes, when Hurston returned in September she brushed him off. By December she would no longer see him at all.

Hughes was unaware that Hurston had sent critic Carl Van Vechten the play to read. Without Hurston's consent, Van Vechten sent the script on to a playhouse in Cleveland called The Theater Guild. While the first script did only have Hurston's name at the top, it is questionable whether she really was trying to pass the work off as her own. When it was sent off for a copyright, it had both author's names on it, although it was now renamed *Mule Bone.*

When Hughes heard the news that the theater had received a script named *Mule Bone* by Zora Neale Hurston, he was furious, thinking she had acted behind his back. Hurston was angry that the script had been passed on without her knowledge. She requested it back immediately. Even so, the situation between the two friends rapidly deteriorated. They bickered about how much of the play each of them had written. When Hurston wired Hughes that no part of the play was his, he hired a lawyer in New York to protect his rights.

"I think it would be lovely for your client to be a playwright," Hurston wrote Hughes's lawyer. "But I'm afraid I am too tight to make him one at my expense. You have written plays, why not do him one yourself? . . . But never no play of mine."

Mutual friends eventually smoothed the relationship

between Hurston and Hughes. Hurston's claim to sole owner-ship melted away, but tensions still filled the air. She finally expressed her resentment over Thompson. Hughes also attributed her behavior to nerves and the stress of getting her folklore collections ready for publication.

Another one of the complicating factors throughout the situation was Mason's patronage, always a thorn in both writers' sides. Her personality brought pressures on both Hurston and Hughes. Hughes had grown increasingly uneasy about her funding. Plagued by psychosomatic symptoms, by December he had returned to his home in Cleveland, and left Mason's payroll. As soon as Mason's money was out of his pocket, Hughes's symptoms abated. Hurston also chafed under Mason's view of African Americans as "primitives." While Hurston could play this role when she needed something from Mason, she was growing tired of this game. However, Hurston was trapped as Mason still paid for Thompson to type her folklore collections.

Then overnight Hurston learned that Thompson had vis-ited Hughes in Cleveland. Although their visit had nothing to do with the play, Hurston was convinced they were schem-ing together. After berating Hughes she left for New York, accusing him of double-crossing her. Attempts by friends failed to patch up the quarrel this time.

Mule Bone was performed in Cleveland on February 15, 1931, but the actors soon voted to discontinue it because of production problems. Only the third act of the play was ever published. It had become notorious for the sole reason that it destroyed Hurston and Hughes's relationship. The two close friends became lifelong enemies. Hughes never forgave Hurston for what he considered to be her theft and dishonesty. She accused him of stealing her ideas and sabotaging the play. The bitterness and pain stayed with both writers; they avoided each other for the rest of their lives. While these years were ones of regret and sorrow for Hurston, they were also times of great creative energy and zest for her life and her work.

five

Stories and songs

n the spring of 1931 Hurston began to seek out theatri-
cal people to present folklore. The stage could breathe
life into the sweet and sorrowful songs and the rhyth-
mic dances she had seen. She met with producer Forbes
Randolph and wrote three sketches for his revue *Fast and
Furious*. However, the show folded in one week. Instead
of making five hundred dollars, like she'd hoped, Hurston
made seventy-five dollars. Again she turned to Godmother
for financial support. After a second failed revue, Hurston
dreamed of one that would hold true to folk traditions. She
tentatively titled it *Spunk*. Hurston took her musical material to Hal Johnson, one of the most famous choral direc-
tors in the country. After several months he returned the
songs, saying they were not well enough arranged or styl-
ized. Hurston, who wanted the music to be authentic, took
this as a personal challenge.

Hurston demonstrating the traditional "Crow Dance" *(Courtesy of Prentiss Taylor, reprinted with permission of Roderick Quiroz, Yale Collection of American Literature, Beinecke Rare Book and Manuscript Library)*

Within six months Hurston had rounded up a group of singers and dancers for her own revue, now called *The Great Day*. Many of the performers were immigrants with colorful names like "Motor Boat" and "Stew Meat" from Bimini Island in the Bahamas. They practiced in her apartment, singing work songs, playing kids' games, and performing dances. When Hurston decided that *The Great Day* was ready, she took it to Johnson. He agreed to try it on stage, but ultimately their agreement fell apart. She claimed he stole material from her and that the end of one of his plays was just like her grand finale.

The setback only fueled Hurston's determination. Although on March 31, 1931, Hurston had ended her prickly

Hurston (far right) stands on stage during a rehearsal with the cast of *The Great Day*. *(Courtesy of the Stetson Kennedy Foundation Collection, Zora Neale Hurston Collection, George A. Smathers Libraries, University of Florida, Department of Special Collections)*

relationship with Mason, she now turned to her again for financial backing. Hurston spent two hundred dollars on ads for the musical, and another $250 on costumes. She sold her car in order to put a deposit down on the theater and pawned her radio to pay for the performers' subway tokens. The play's first performance was an artistic success. Hurston exclaimed, "The world wanted to hear the glorious voice of my people."

But *The Great Day* remained far from a financial success. Hurston was mired in debt to Mason to the tune of $610.00. She had hoped a Broadway producer would take an interest in the play, but none did. Mason also technically held the rights over the songs and the dances. She disapproved of revues and wanted this material published in books instead. Hurston wanted the character and the color of the songs and dances to shine on stage. She also needed to develop this material to pay off her loan. The pair hammered out a legal agreement in 1932 detailing certain material for theatrical purposes. Other material was only for Godmother-approved purposes. For financial reasons, Hurston still had to toe the line and walk the perils of patronage. However, *The Great Day* would live on to see more performances. For the next three years it would earn Hurston money and fame, helping her to earn a bit of a living while she continued to write.

On April 28, 1932, Hurston's Godmother helped her again. Hesitantly, Mason agreed to finance another trip south for Hurston to continue working on her folktales. Hurston had train fare and a pair of new shoes, helpful because her big toe had burst through her only pair. This time Mason demanded that Hurston submit a detailed expense account of her spending. Hurston complied, sending Mason a list of items she'd bought along the way, including string beans, canned fruit, and colon medicine.

By late May Hurston was home in Eatonville, back to her garden and writing. The change in scenery helped her creativity to flow. She planted a garden full of watermelon, beans, okra, and black-eye peas. By day she revised her work, by night she sat on the porch listening to the songs of mockingbirds.

Within two months, as the weather grew hotter and drier, Hurston typed and finished *Mules and Men*. Her writing ability shone clearly. She wrote for the average reader, not for the scientific community. Each of the seventy folktales began with Hurston easing the reader into different surroundings. With her creative reporting style, she conveyed the artistic significance of the folklore. However, Hurston had struggled to shape the book. Even so she soldiered on.

"I shall wrassle me up a future, or die trying," Hurston said of her attempts.

Hurston had shown various drafts to Mason although the manuscript had been mainly completed two years earlier. Her imagination had been checked by Mason as she wrote about traditions that weren't anyone's to purchase.

Finally Hurston sent *Mules and Men* out to publishers, hoping to find her manuscript a home. While publishers offered her ideas for revision, no one was ready to publish it yet. Mason grew increasingly frustrated and less patient with the rejections. Waiting to hear from publishers would require patience.

Hurston kept busy in central Florida. She recast *The Great Day* as the play *From Sun to Sun* in different Florida cities. However producing shows was not a steady well-paying job in central Florida. Hurston turned again to fiction, which she had not written for nearly six years. Again out from Mason's umbrella of patronage, she was getting a bit desperate for money. Hurston was just one of the Great Depression's many unemployed.

Few federal financial aid programs existed, and only a limited number of states had small welfare funds. There was no unemployment insurance. Public housing did not exist until early in the 1930s. In 1932, financially strapped Americans pinned their hopes on Franklin Delano Roosevelt, the presidential candidate who promised a "new deal for America." Roosevelt won in a landslide victory over Herbert Hoover,

Franklin Delano Roosevelt *(Library of Congress)*

and his promises of a fresh start won him the majority of the black vote. When Roosevelt took office in 1933, he immediately began working on a series of programs and policies known as the New Deal, to hoist the country out of its financial depression.

Roosevelt conducted his first one hundred days in office at a feverish pace. He sent several pieces of legislation to

Congress to help factories, farms, banks, and the millions of unemployed people. One of his relief programs was the WPA or Works Progress Administration. This administration hired out-of-work farmers and factory workers to build schools, pave roads, and erect bridges. Artists and writers especially benefited from the WPA. They had found it nearly impossible to continue their creative works, until the federal government stepped in. The government hired artists to paint murals in public buildings such as libraries and museum, writers to produce thousands of publications, including state and city guidebooks, musicians to produce symphonies, and actors to stage plays. Gradually, through his administration's new regulations for banks and his government programs, Roosevelt was beginning to instill confidence again.

Despite the slow lifting of the veil of the Great Depression, Hurston needed a boost. Early in 1933 her sister Sarah, who had been living in New Jersey, died of pneumonia. She was forty-three years old. Also in New York Godmother was hospitalized indefinitely. The eighty-year-old woman had taken a nasty fall and broken her hip.

Two items gave Hurston solace. The first was her niece and namesake. After Hurston's sister's death, various relatives passed around Sarah's daughter. For three years she traveled between houses, much like Hurston had when her mother had died. For a few months she lived with her sympathetic Aunt Zora who often cooked meals for the pair and managed to buy her niece "the most gorgeous clothes" and "beautiful things" on her meager earnings. Hurston's other solace in her times of trouble was to turn to her paper and pencil.

She attempted a fresh story about slave ship survivor Cudjo Lewis, about whom she'd written years earlier. The story "Barracoon" only met with rejections. Hurston was frustrated and sapped by problems with her tonsils.

Her ailments left her feeling "only half of me at least a third of the time," Hurston said.

Hurston focused and wrote another short story. She sent the story "The Gilded Six-Bits" to Robert Wunsch, a professor in the English department at Rollins College near Eatonville. The story is considered one of Hurston's best. It is a tale of infidelity, sorrow, and forgiveness. The story begins with Missie May and Joe Banks, a happily married couple. Then Missie May succumbs to the advances of Otis D. Slemmons in exchange for gold for Joe. However Joe discovers the pair, and the gold turns out to only be a gilded half dollar. Joe carries the coin with him as a reminder, but slowly the couple heals.

Wunsch liked the tale. He read it to his English class and sent it to the editors of *Story* magazine. The magazine published it in August of 1933. Hurston received letters from four publishers asking if she had any books they could consider for publication. The letter from publisher Bertram Lippincott from the J. B. Lippincott Company appealed most to Hurston. She wrote back telling Lippincott that she was working on a novel.

"Mind you, not the first word was on paper when I wrote him that letter," Hurston admitted later.

Lippincott's expressed interest lit a fire under Hurston. The next week she moved to Sanford, Florida, where she could concentrate in surroundings that were less comfortable and familiar. She lived on fifty cents a week, which her cousin lent her for groceries. She wrote on a card table in a one room house, rented for $1.50 a week. On July 1,

Hurston began the book *Jonah's Gourd Vine*. By September 6 she had finished and borrowed two dollars to mail it to Lippincott. On October 16, Hurston got her first stroke of good luck in a while. She received a letter of acceptance, and the offer of a two hundred dollar advance. The letter came just in time, as Hurston's landlord had evicted her that morning for owing rent money. Hurston had opened the publisher's telegram while she was buying shoes to replace her old leather ones, which were in scraps. When she saw the amount of the advance she, "tore out of the place with one old shoe and one new one on and ran to the Western Union office," to accept the offer. The book was published in early May of 1934.

Jonah's Gourd Vine parallels Hurston's life: her father's pursuit of other women, her mother's strength, and her mother's deathbed scene. The tale begins with her father John's story—a man's rise from an Alabama plantation to the Eatonville ministry, however he cannot resist women. After his wife dies, this fault worsens and his congregation rejects him. He dies just as he understands his successes and failures. Hurston used this novel as vehicle to portray her father as a Christian poet with extraordinary talent.

Reporters praised *Jonah's Gourd Vine*. Critic Martha Gruening of the *New Republic* wrote that the story was the "most vital and original novel about the American Negro that has been written be a member of the Negro race." However, many reviewers missed Hurston's point about John Hurston's poetic ability.

With one published novel under her belt, finding a home for *Mules and Men* now became easier. Lippincott published the book in 1935.

Mary McLeod Bethune *(Library of Congress)*

Hurston soon discovered that a two hundred dollar advance didn't last long. She started looking for a steady job. Her work with the play *From Sun to Sun* had brought her to the attention of Mary McLeod Bethune. Bethune was the president of Bethune-Cookman College in Daytona Beach, Florida. Mary McLeod Bethune was one of the most famous African American women in the United States. She had founded the National Council of Negro Women and built Bethune College from a girls' training school into an accredited college. Soon she would become one of Franklin Delano Roosevelt's advisors.

In December of 1933 she invited Hurston to establish a drama school based on African American expression at her college. An opportunity to teach drama and work with Bethune was not one to pass up.

Soon after Hurston started she was at odds with authority and academics. Never one for stringent rules and bars to her creativity, she soon entered into a contest of wills over writing a pageant for the school's thirtieth anniversary. Both Hurston and Bethune had strong personalities. By April of 1934 Hurston said she had "decided to abandon the farce of Bethune-Cookman's Drama Department and get on with my work."

Sometimes when Hurston needed money, one of her zany money-making schemes emerged. In 1934 she began selling chicken salad, chicken soup, chicken à la king, and hot fried chicken to New York City's finest hostesses. Her idea of niche catering never really took off. Hurston's heart was never in it and soon more promising opportunities were falling into place.

In the fall of 1934 a group from Chicago, Illinois asked her if she would be interested in sponsoring another performance of *The Great Day*. On her way north she stopped in Nashville to give a small concert at Fisk University. The president of the university, Thomas Jones, urged her to apply for a job as a drama professor.

Once in Chicago Hurston led productions of *The Great Day*, along with a new show titled *Singing Steel*. She also continued to give lectures and interviews, covering her costs and living expenses, while staying at a YWCA. Her work again attracted attention. Members of the Julius Rosenwald Foundation invited Hurston to return to Columbia University

Julius Rosenwald *(Library of Congress)*

to study for her PhD in anthropology and folklore. Julius Rosenwald was president of Sears, Roebuck & Company. His foundation improved the lives of millions by donating to hospitals, schools, museums, relief agencies, and research groups. It built and funded more than 5,300 schools for African Americans, along with providing housing for teachers and promoting higher education. This opportunity from the Rosenwald Foundation came just as Fisk University was backing away from its job offer. The university had grown concerned about Hurston's flamboyance and past conflicts at Bethune-Cookman.

Now despite the Great Depression, Hurston had the opportunity to study without any financial worries. It was a prestigious fellowship and university, well known for supporting its black students. The dramatic presentation of folklore had begun to pale for Hurston as it was increasingly frustrating at times. Now with the publication of *Jonah's Gourd Vine* and *Mules and Men*, Hurston hoped a doctoral degree from Columbia might command people to see the thought and traditions behind her work.

Hurston had another interest at Columbia—graduate student Percival McGuire Punter. She had met him in New York in 1931 when he was singing in *The Great Day*. Although he was twenty-three and she was forty-four, the pair stayed up late at night talking about religion, art, and literature. They also enjoyed cooking together. However, Punter disliked Hurston's having a career and became jealous at the demands her career had on her time with him. She began to get up late at night so she could write. Things grew more serious however when Punter asked Hurston to marry him and leave New York. Marrying and leaving New York was fine, but giving up her career was one thing Hurston could not do.

Hurston said:

> I really wanted to do anything he wanted me to do, but that one thing I could not do. I had things clawing inside of me that must be said. I could not see that my work should make any difference in marriage. He was all and everything else to me but that . . . But it was different with him. He felt that he did not matter to me enough. He was the master kind. All, or nothing, for him.

Even so Hurston had a difficult time breaking away. They continued to see each other, despite increasing conflict and jealousies. On top of this emotional wringer Hurston weighed her fellowship offer.

The Rosenwald Foundation originally offered Hurston three thousand dollars over two years. Then in a series of changes between Hurston and the foundation, the deals changed. The foundation reneged on its original offer, saying her degree plan was unacceptable, even though Franz Boas had drawn it up with her and agreed to direct her. Constraints, limitations, and amounts kept changing. Finally, a frustrated Hurston took off on a short collecting and writing tour after accepting the fellowship. Each party was never able to fully iron out details, and it was Hurston's final break with folklore as an academic subject. This abrupt trip also helped to sever ties between she and Punter.

By August of 1935 Hurston was back in New York City for the October release of *Mules and Men*. Reviews of the book were mixed, as with many of Hurston's works. Some black intellectuals argued that the book didn't tell the truth to white Americans as it didn't express bitterness and anger at racial injustice and suppression. Hurston did not deal with this resentment and injustice. To her that was history, not folklore. Her work shows laughing and living, just like everyone else, despite racial problems.

Soon Hurston again had little money, so she looked for work with the Works Progress Administration (WPA). The WPA Federal Theater Project hired her at $23.86 a week to work as a drama coach. She stayed through March 20, 1936. Shortly after Hurston left the WPA theater, it staged its most famous production. Director Orson Welles led an all-black cast in a production of *Macbeth*, set in Haiti.

On January 6, 1937, Hurston received wonderful news. She had applied for funding from the John Simon Guggenheim Memorial Foundation, which provides grants of money for scholars and artists in fields such as the arts, humanities, and sciences. Hurston had proposed to study the African roots of voudou and black cultural practices in the United States. In her application she emphasized that her "ultimate purpose as a student is to increase the general knowledge concerning my people, but in the Negro way and away from the white man's way."

The Guggenheim Foundation offered Hurston two years of funding. She planned to focus on studying voudou in Jamaica and Haiti. She dove into writing and collecting folklore once again. She spent six months in Jamaica, mostly with the Maroons, a group of people who had fought their way out of slavery in the 1650s. Living high in the mountains of west Jamaica, Hurston witnessed their rituals and observed their uses of medicinal plants.

Hurston plays a drum she brought back from a folklore-gathering trip to Haiti. *(Library of Congress)*

Hurston eagerly adapted to life in the mountains, dwelling in thatched huts, and watching centuries-old songs and dances. The women cooked over open fires. When Hurston discovered that the village had no cooking stove, she designed and help build one out of tin, cement, and stovepipe. "We were really joyful," Hurston said, "when we fired it the next day and found out that it worked."

From Jamaica Hurston traveled on to Haiti. Here she learned more about voudou gods, differentiating between the Petro gods and Rada gods. The wicked and feared Petro gods required great sacrifice, while the milder Rada gods required only small animal sacrifices. People informed Hurston that as a foreign woman she would need a guide. She confidently laughed off the idea, until she saw a man supposedly possessed by a Petro spirit. She quickly decided a guide was worth the price.

Soon she arrived at the Île de la Gonâve, near the harbor of Port-au-Prince, Haiti. The locals believed that a whale with a sleepy goddess on its back had formed this island. The goddess possessed the formula for peace in her hands. The legend, the glittering sea, the lush green foliage, and the misty air enchanted Hurston. Haiti released in her a flood of language. Hurston moved into a small house in the hills and for the next seven weeks wrote until late in the evening. By the third week of December she had finished her second novel. She titled it *Their Eyes Were Watching God*. The novel had tumbled out of her as she once again drew on her personal experiences, remembering loves and losses. Memories of the rolling sea and whipping winds from the hurricane years earlier in the Bahamas helped stir Hurston's imagination for parts of *Their Eyes Were Watching God*.

However in June of 1937, while living in this remote area, she became violently ill. "For a day and night I'd thought I'd never make it," she wrote a friend later. She lay in bed for two weeks and was eventually carried to the United States consul who paid for her trip home. Spooked, Hurston was convinced that her illness and voudou studies were related. She had learned many harmful voudou practices, such as placing finely chopped horse hair in food to kill somebody. The use of plants and poisons both fascinated and terrified her. "The greatest power of voudou rests upon poisons and their antidotes," she wrote.

Whether Hurston had the flu, an intestinal disorder, or was poisoned, she would never know. Either way she backed off of her work, frightened and shaken by what she had seen and experienced. She planned to finish her work at home, fleshing out the voudou rituals she had collected into her next book. She planned to title it *Tell My Horse,* after the powerful god Guedé, who drinks rum and hot pepper. The god invisibly takes over people, as if they were his horse, and makes them do his bidding. Hurston happily and hastily returned home, to dwell on the tales of Guedé and other powerful rituals from the safe pages of her notes, rather than in the midst of the swirling voudou practices and beliefs.

six

Up the Peaky Mountains

When Hurston returned to the United States, life took an upswing. Lippincott had quickly snapped up *Their Eyes Were Watching God* with little revision. They made plans to publish the story in the fall of 1937. Beautiful powerful images of nature punctuate the stormy love story based on Hurston's doomed relationship with Punter.

In *Their Eyes Were Watching God* Hurston tells the tale of Janie Crawford. Punter was the prototype for the male character Tea Cake, and his tender, although ultimately impossible, relationship, with Janie. In writing the story Hurston discovered that it was primarily men who told the lies on Joe Clarke's porch so many years ago on those steamy summer afternoons. Through Janie, Hurston explored women's rights to tell a story and to have a private self. Many readers today wonder if Hurston was reconciling her public career with her private emotion in this book.

As *Their Eyes Were Watching God* opens, Janie had grown up under her grandmother's care. The older woman wishes for Janie to be spared the traditional wife's beast-of-burden role. She wants Janie to be more like the white women she sees who sit on the porch and don't have to work. She marries Janie to Logan Killicks, a man who turns out to be heartless and cruel, despite his appearance. Janie leaves him for Joe Starks. When Starks passes away, young Janie publicly revolts against mourning traditions and falls in love with Vergible "Tea Cake" Woods, a young, free-spirited laborer. Janie works beside him, having realized that she doesn't like sitting on a throne of a porch. In contrast to Janie's past relationships, Tea Cake is a strong, open, and giving partner. When a hurricane comes, he saves Janie, but is bitten by a rabid dog. When Tea Cake contracts the disease and goes mad, he attempts to shoot Janie. In a tragic end she is forced to shoot her love in self defense and is acquitted by a white jury.

In many ways *Their Eyes Were Watching God* illustrates Hurston's philosophies. Just as Janie dislikes being on her throne, Hurston believed people erred by wanting to be above others. It denied the humanity of those below them in society or wealth. She believed black people became truly free, not by emulating whites, but by building the cultural institutions of their own community. Janie and Tea Cake also illustrate Hurston's belief that relationships between men and women are strongest when equal and with mutual consent and status.

Many reviewers praised *Their Eyes Were Watching God* for its powerful sensory imagery and the tale that Hurston

The cover of an early edition of *Their Eyes Were Watching God* (*Courtesy of Yale Collection of American Literature, Beinecke Rare Book and Manuscript Library*)

spun. Lucy Tompkins wrote for the *New York Times Book Review,* "from the first to last this is well-nigh a perfect story, but the rest is simple and beautiful and shining with humor." Others attacked the book, saying it simply perpetuated stereotypes. Her old professor Alain Locke called it folklore fiction, saying the story wasn't modern enough and didn't any have social value. Characteristic of her temper, Hurston angrily fired off a malicious description of Locke. Although Locke had often helped her, his criticism frustrated and hurt her. Hurston's work and talents often fell short of acclaim because her writing was not seen as being confrontational, at a time when many African Americans hungered for writing that promoted an end to racial injustices. Hurston's attitudes were her own, with a unique spin.

Racism confounded Hurston. She acknowledged that "sometimes I feel discriminated against, but it does not make me angry. It merely astonishes me. How can any deny themselves the pleasure of my company! It's beyond me."

The tone of Hurston's writings was often out of step with the mood of the country. Fellow African American author Richard Wright had better success. Based on his vision of black life, Wright wrote about the horrors of racism. The tales of despair matched the country's emotions at the time. Wright's book *Native Son* landed on the Book of the Month Club list, was made into a movie, and sold 300,000 copies, while Hurston's book *Their Eyes Were Watching God* sold 5,000 copies. By the early 1940s Hurston was out of creative step with other black writers, although that had never bothered her before. She had always moved and written to a different beat.

By March of 1938 Hurston had also completed her next book, *Tell My Horse*. She finished hastily, almost in an attempt to put voudou behind her. The book debuted in October to kind reviews. However the mix of style and subject matter did not sell well. Hurston had attempted to be a novelist and a folklorist. As well as tales, Hurston had sprinkled naïve political analysis and generalizations throughout the book.

Perhaps the darkest section of *Tell My Horse* was when Hurston recounts her encounter with a zombie. A government doctor had chillingly warned her that learning about zombies might "cost you more than you are willing to pay." Hurston cautiously described her findings. She told of her visit to a hospital in Haiti where she photographed a female zombie named Felicia Felix-Mentor. The woman had died and been buried in 1907. Then nearly thirty years later she was found wandering on the road, without the power of speech. "If science ever gets to the bottom of voudou in Haiti and Africa," Hurston wrote, "it will be found that some important medical secrets, still unknown to medical science give it its power, rather than the gestures of ceremony."

After writing about zombies Hurston turned to tamer projects. While living in Florida, she got a job as an editor with the Federal Writers' Project, a government organization started by President Roosevelt's wife, Eleanor, to provide unemployed authors with jobs during the Great Depression.

The fog of the Great Depression was slowly lifting, aided by the United States's involvement in World War II. From 1935 to 1937 Congress had passed a series of neutrality acts to isolate the country from the growing European conflict. Then in March of 1939 German chancellor Adolf Hitler defied the Munich Pact by invading the rest of Czechoslovakia. Britain

Felicia Felix-Mentor *(Courtesy of Mary Evans Picture Library/Alamy)*

and Germany had made the pact a year earlier, allowing Germany to extend its territory into parts of Czechoslovakia with German-speaking people. Soon Hitler also sent troops into Poland causing Great Britain and France to declare war on Germany. Within the next two years the Nazi war machine swallowed up Denmark, Norway, Holland, Belgium, and France. In the face of such aggression, the United States began sending weapons and war supplies to European allies. To meet the needs of supplying Europe, factories stepped up production, creating more goods and more jobs. From 1938 to 1942 the average income of a family living in Washington, D.C., doubled.

Hurston also found more stable and profitable work through the Federal Writers' Project. Several other black authors found work too, such as Ralph Ellison and Arna Bontemps. Hurston worked in Florida, editing state guidebooks. She worked for the project for about one and a half years, often disappearing for a week or more at a time. Others just assumed she was collecting folklore for the guidebook, but she was actually starting her next book.

In June of 1939 Hurston received an honorary degree from her high school alma mater, Morgan State. She turned to black colleges for employment. Quickly, Dr. James Shepherd, the president of North Carolina College for Negroes, hired her to organize a drama program. Located in Durham, North Carolina, the college was one of the best known schools in the South. Hurston brought national publicity to the school as well.

Around this same time Hurston got married again. On June 27, 1939, she married Albert Price III. He was a twenty-three-year-old college student. Again shifty about her age, Hurston

Hurston stands beside an exhibit for the Federal Works Project in 1938.
(Library of Congress)

gave her birth year as 1910, so she would be twenty-nine and marrying a man slightly younger. In reality she was at least thirty-eight years old. They had met in Jacksonville, Florida, where he was a playground worker for the Works Progress Administration. Their courtship had been brief. Quickly it became apparent that Hurston had made the wrong decision in marrying Price. Their age difference and personalities were divisive.

Beyond her recent marriage, Hurston celebrated release of a new work, *Moses, Man of the Mountain,* a book that she had been working on for many years. Lippincott published the title in November of 1939. Five years earlier she had written a short story about Moses and the legends surrounding him for the literary magazine *Challenge*. Recent historical evidence published by Sigmund Freud had suggested that Moses was Egyptian rather than Hebrew. Hurston now claimed he was African, citing his stature in the Mediterranean and Africa.

"Wherever the children of Africa have been scattered by slavery, there is the acceptance of Moses as the fountain of mystic power," Hurston wrote.

Black spirituals often refer to Moses traveling to Egypt and telling the pharaoh to "let my people go." Moses then leads the chosen people to freedom. African Americans highly identified with these elements of slavery and captivity, as history told of Egyptian masters decreeing the death of all Jewish infants.

While Hurston's *Moses, Man of the Mountain* might have fallen short of her expectations, the book is a fascinating, but uncertain, blend of biblical tone, dialect, humor, and reference to legend. The book was an immense aspiration from the start. Never one to shirk from an insurmountable task, falling victim to her huge undertakings would begin to plague Hurston. Depressing reviews began to trickle in.

To make matters worse, Hurston's work at the college was not progressing smoothly. As she did with most rule makers, she soon crossed swords with the college president. He expected his faculty members to live on campus and to not make waves. Hurston instead lived in a cabin in the mountains so she had solitude to write. She also arrived each day in a flashy red convertible. Hurston complained about her class schedule and was inconsistent in her teaching. Through many differences of opinion there were no plays that year at the college. Soon both parties gladly parted ways with little regret.

In February of 1940 Hurston filed for a divorce from her new husband, saying he drank, refused to work, and was often abusive. Price denied her claims, instead saying Hurston dragged him to the altar, promising that her income would enable him to continue his college education. The truth most likely lies somewhere in between. For a brief time Hurston and Price reconciled, but in reality their marriage lasted less than a year. By late summer of 1940 they parted for good; their divorce was granted three years later.

Hurston returned to New York for the winter of 1940 to 1941. She gave lectures and visited with old friends. Hurston mulled possibilities for another book. She had reported on folklore. She had written two novels based on Eatonville. She also had made an unsuccessful stab at writing biblical fiction. Her publisher now suggested Hurston write her autobiography.

Hurston listens to songs while collecting stories in Eatonville, Florida, in 1935. *(Library of Congress)*

In the late spring of 1941 Hurston moved to California, at the urging of Katharine Edson Mershon. Mershon was a modern dancer and fellow anthropologist who had studied and recorded the rituals and traditions in Bali. Mershon lived in California and was anxious for some intellectual company. Like Hurston she had published a book based on her findings. With such common ground, Mershon offered Hurston a place in her California home to live and write. The pair traveled throughout California together, visiting towering redwood forests, deserts, cable cars, and colorful fishermen's wharves.

By the middle of July Hurston had finished the first draft of her autobiography. She found the format difficult and spent a year revising and reworking. Her work was inconsistent and she was self conscious. Her first nineteen years had been full of personal and professional disappointments.

"I did not want to write it at all," Hurston said of the book, "because it is too hard to reveal one's inner self."

At the time Hurston also was having a difficult time keeping her political feelings out of her work. The United States was involved in the European front of World War II and relations were worsening with Japan. Then on December 7, 1941, the Japanese bombed the U.S. naval base at Pearl Harbor, Hawaii. The losses were devastating for the unprepared navy. The sneak attack on the base near Honolulu killed more than 22,000 men and destroyed more than two hundred American aircraft. The United States fully joined World War II. For the next four years the fight against Japan and Germany had the advantage of creating 17 million new jobs for the country. As factories churned out uniforms, blankets, ships, and planes, there were more jobs than workers. Millions of women filled jobs that formerly had been occupied by men, after husbands, fathers, and sons were drafted. Now women worked at jobs such as welding and operating heavy equipment.

Like any other American Hurston had her own feelings about the war, but always more of a writer than a politician she was unable to express her views clearly in her book. She condemned missionary work and organized religion saying it undermined the beliefs of people of color around the world. She spoke out against France, Germany, England, and the United States for their imperialist attitudes over Asia, Africa, and Latin America. Often her views seemed contradictory.

Eventually, editors deleted many of her rambling passages on international and racial issues.

After traveling to lecture at several different black colleges, Hurston returned to St. Augustine, Florida. There she lived on her meager savings, dabbled in writing a few plays, and polished her autobiography. The resulting book, entitled *Dust Tracks on a Road,* was published in late November of 1942.

Lippincott published *Dust Tracks on a Road* at the height of Hurston's career and popularity as a writer. Overall the book met with success. At times, the tales contained within are larger-than-life, but they give a glimpse of Hurston's public and private life. It tells the story of her life—from her early beginnings to her high climbs.

"I have been in Sorrow's kitchen and licked out all the pots," she writes. "Then I have stood on the peaky mountains wrapped in rainbows with a harp and a sword in my hands." For the moment Hurston stood atop the peaky mountains.

seven

In Sorrow's Kitchen

With the success of her autobiography, Hurston continued to drive herself to write. She also began teaching at a local black college, Florida Normal. But like her last attempts at teaching, Hurston soon quarreled with the administration. Never one to avoid a fight, she threw her weight behind a group of servicemen being trained at the school when they complained about the college president and their living quarters. Troubles with the college persisted and in early 1943 Hurston moved on to Daytona Beach, Florida. With her slight savings from teaching and writing, she purchased a twenty-year-old house boat named *Wanago*. Crammed full of her books and papers, the boat was the perfect place of solitude. Hurston, who loved the weather and water, found her new floating home perfect. The boat also served as a base for fishing, a hobby she loved. For the next four years she happily traveled up and down Florida's Indian and Halifax Rivers.

Dust Tracks on the Road won the Anisfield-Wolf Book Award, a tribute recognizing books that make a contribution to understanding racism or appreciating cultural diversity. Hurston also appeared on the cover of the "Saturday Review of Literature." She was the first black author honored this way. She also was awarded the annual distinguished alumni award from Howard University and joined the Florida Negro Defense Committee.

In the meantime, Hurston became engaged to James Howell Pitts, a forty-five-year-old Cleveland, Ohio businessman. Originally from South Carolina, Pitts had a degree in pharmacy from Meharry Medical College. How Hurston and Pitts met isn't clear. Hurston had been in Ohio in February of 1939 promoting her work, but she'd been in southwestern Ohio. Pitts did give his address on the marriage documents as Brunswick, Georgia, about 160 miles from Daytona Beach, so it's possible they met in the South. Hurston claimed she was forty, although in reality she was fifty-three. The couple married on January 18, 1944, in Duval County, Florida. They married one year after Hurston's divorce from Price was finalized. Within weeks of her marriage to Pitts she returned to New York for work. Eight months later, in October of 1944, Hurston's third marriage ended when the couple divorced.

In the meantime, an exciting new prospect loomed on Hurston's horizon. Reginald Brett, an English mining engineer had contacted her. He had recently returned to the United States after mining for gold for several years in Honduras. Hurston's book *Tell My Horse* had impressed Brett. He suggested she come along on a research trip, offering the

Hurston (front) sits in a boat during an expedition to collect folklore.
(Courtesy of the Stetson Kennedy Foundation Collection, Zora Neale Hurston Collection, George A. Smathers Libraries, University of Florida, Department of Special Collections)

promise that Honduras brimmed with undiscovered folklore. He also claimed he was the only person to have laid eyes on an ancient Mayan city. The lure of an exciting anthropological scoop on a mysterious lost city appealed to Hurston, along with the wealth and fame associated with such a find.

Hurston convinced Fred Irvine, a Miami seaman and adventurer, to let her charter his boat for her research. Irvine, an Englishman, would do the sailing for free. In return she promised to pay for provisions, minor repairs, new sails, and a new paint job for his twenty-seven-ton schooner, the *Maridome*. However, she still didn't have enough money to buy a recording machine and to fund the research expedition, despite her exhausting search for financial support.

Although Hurston's eyes were still set toward Honduras in 1945 she replaced her weather-beaten boat with a new one named the *Sun Tan*. She had sold her car and many other items to pay for her end of her deal with Irvine. She lounged on her boat, taking in the sun, and sometimes eating a dozen oranges at a sitting. As always she continued to write. But in September Lippincott rejected her latest book, *Mrs. Doctor.* Hurston attempted revisions, but her sloppy work surprised editors. She shelved the project.

Nonplussed, Hurston turned her attention to other directions. In the spring of 1947, her friend Marjorie Kinnan Rawlings smoothed the road. Hurston met Rawlings while living in Saint Augustine. She had invited the fellow author to speak to her class at Florida Normal. In 1939 Rawlings had won the Pulitzer Prize for her novel *The Yearling,* a story of a boy who adopts an orphaned fawn. She published nine other books, eight dealing with Florida. After speaking to Hurston's class, Rawlings had invited her to tea at her

Marjorie Kinnan Rawlings *(Library of Congress)*

husband's segregated resort hotel. Although Rawlings gave special orders to the elevator man to take Hurston to their residence, Hurston knew how life worked in the South. She entered through the kitchen and walked up the stairs.

With that first visit, the two became friends with a shared love of writing and of living and working in rural Florida. Now at Rawling's suggestion Hurston switched publishers to Charles Scribner's Sons. After a few meetings Hurston had a deal for her next novel and a $500 advance. She knew exactly what to do with the money.

On May 4 Hurston set sail for Puerto Cortés, the bustling Honduran port city on the north coast. She sailed on a commercial liner, as Irvine had moved on after two years. She stayed at the Hotel Cosenza, as gray manatees bobbed in the sea and iguanas climbed in the nearby jungle cloud forests. By the summer Hurston was out of money and still hadn't glimpsed the ancient city. Scribner's gave her another five hundred dollar advance, with which Hurston hoped to do more exploring and writing.

In September Hurston mailed the draft of a manuscript to New York. She had titled the book *Good Morning Son*. Editing stretched into December, the rainy season in Honduras, so there was no exploring. Rain lashed the country, eighteen inches falling in three days. Scribner's wired Hurston money to come to New York for the final edit of the book. They set a day of October 11, 1948, for the book to come out. During the editing process Hurston had thanked Burroughs Mitchell, an editor at Scribner's, for his keen attention to detail.

"Please remember that I am neither Moses nor any of the writing apostles. Nothing that I set down is sacred," she said.

"Any word or sentence can be changed or even cut out. What we want is success, not my deification."

After editing, the book was retitled *Seraph on the Suwanee* and the story told of a family of poor white Southerners. Hurston follows the life and marriage of her two main characters, Arvay Henson Meserve and Jim Meserve. Jim is strong and handsome, but also deeply chauvinistic. He ultimately becomes a shrimp boat captain to support his family, while Arvay worries that she won't be able to hold onto her wonderful husband. He abuses his power over his devoted wife. Although they love each other deeply, the roles that they box themselves into lead to an unhappy ending. Arvay realizes that as little as she has known Jim, she knew herself even less. Hurston had presented marriage as a death of personality and individuality. In Hurston's life she herself had rejected marriage three times now. *Seraph on the Suwanee* offers some of her reasoning.

After Hurston returned to New York, many things changed in her world. Her Harlem years were long gone. On April 15, 1946, her old patron Godmother had passed away. The world too was different, following the country's involvement in World War II. Hurston steadfastly remained the same despite the differences in the world around her. She was true to herself and stout in her beliefs, but soon her faith in her fellow humans would be tested.

On September 13, 1948, police pounded on the door of Hurston's New York apartment. They arrested her on charges that she had sexually molested a ten-year-old boy. Hurston had rented a room from the boy's mother two years earlier. The claim was false. Hurston had been in Honduras at the time of the alleged incident. However no one listened at first to her alibi.

Burroughs Mitchell, her Scribner's editor, secretly bailed Hurston out of jail. She quietly moved to an apartment in the Bronx, a northern area of New York City. Next, she hired lawyer Louis Waldman. Three weeks later the court indicted Hurston based on the boy's testimony. She was both outraged and filled with despair. "My country has failed me utterly," she wrote, feeling that her reputation had been destroyed.

Armed with Hurston's passport, her lawyer took her case to the District Attorney of Manhattan, Frank Hogan. The passport provided dates and evidence refuting the boy's claims. Hogan investigated further and discovered that the child was emotionally disturbed. Hurston had once suggested to the mother that she take her son for psychiatric testing. The mother, who resented Hurston's comment, had seen this charge as a way to exact revenge.

Although the case against Hurston was dismissed, the damage had been done. A national black newspaper, Baltimore, Maryland's *Afro-American*, had given the story lurid front-page coverage. Hurston was devastated and depressed.

The soothing orange groves and sunshine of Florida called her home to Miami in July of 1949. She and her friend Fred Irvine made plans to travel together, and Hurston leaped at the opportunity to escape. Irvine had acquired a new boat, *The Challenger*. The pair took a calm cruise to the Bahamas. After returning to Miami, they decided to travel together to Honduras, like originally planned. For the next five months they slowly prepared. As Hurston waited for the Honduras trip to begin she sunned on Miami Beach and floated in the Biscayne Bay. In the mornings she picked coconuts knocked loose by the wind and met colorful characters.

"God keeps His appointment with Miami every sundown," Hurston wrote. "I get the benefit of His slashing paintbrush all the way. The show is changed every day, but every performance is superb." Slowly Hurston's wounds began to heal, and she started to sound more like herself.

"Day by day in every way I'm getting human again," she wrote Carl Van Vechten. "I caught myself laughing fit to kill yesterday."

Unfortunately though, just as money woes often plagued Hurston, Irvine had the same problem, exacerbated by his gambling. By January of 1950 he was forced to sell off his boat. Hurston, having little money herself, left and began work on her new novel *The Lives of Barney Turk*. The story tells of a southern man who travels through Honduras and has many adventures during his journey.

"Nagged by the necessity of living," Hurston took a job as a maid. She received thirty dollars each week, plus room and board. When her employers discovered her identity, they were shocked, but couldn't keep the story to themselves.

"For the first time in my life I found myself going into my kitchen to hear my maid talk," said Mrs. Kenneth Burritt, Hurston's employer.

A reporter from the *Miami Herald* newspaper knocked on Mrs. Burritt's door to get the scoop on her maid. Hurston filled him with tales and admitted she was taking a writing hiatus.

"I was born with a skillet in my hands," Hurston told him. "I like to cook and clean and keep house. Why shouldn't I do it for somebody else a while. A writer has to stop writing every now and then and just live a little."

The newspaper publicity made Miami aware of Hurston, but even so her financial struggles were taking their toll.

A 1939 photo of Hurston in Cross City,
Florida *(Photo by Stetson Kennedy, Aycock & Lindsay
Turpentine Plantation, Cross City, Fla. 1939/ Stetson
Kennedy Foundation Collection, Zora Neale Hurston
Collection, George A. Smathers Libraries, University of
Florida, Department. of Special Collections)*

She attempted a story titled "Mrs. Doctor" about upper-class African Americans, but it was rejected before it was even finished on the basis that people weren't ready to read about high-class African Americans. Hurston was frustrated with the perils and constrictions of publishers, especially the relationships between white publishers and black authors. In April of 1950 she wrote an essay for *Negro Digest* titled "What White Publishers Won't Print." Hurston was moving toward a career change, dropping the folklore material that had been the substance of her art. It was a heavy price to pay for publication.

Hurston was stunned when her editor had passed on *The Lives of Barney Turk.* He said there was not enough Zora Neale Hurston in it. Her editor encouraged her to turn away from fiction for a while and write a second volume of her autobiography.

But Hurston wasn't willing to dive into the recent events of her life and publish them. In the meantime Hurston sold the article "Why the Negro Won't Buy Communism" to *American Legion Magazine.* Next she tried to expand one of her short stories titled "The Golden Bench of God" into serialization for a women's magazine. The story was based on the life of black hair care stylist Madame C. J. Walker and her daughter A'Leila, whom Hurston had known in Harlem. Hurston sent it to her literary agent Jean Parker Waterbury, who urged her to build the idea into a novel. She fretted about her work though.

"I have just not tried to write a novel," Hurston wrote. "Some of the economic kicks I have suffered in the last half year have reached my vitals." Hurston declared that she was "all too weary of going to the post office and turning away cold in hand and having to avoid folks who have made me loans so that I could eat and sleep. The humiliation is getting to be too much for my self respect."

In 1951 Hurston moved back to Eau Gallie, to the cabin where she had written *Mules and Men.* Shortly afterwards she received notice that her attempts on *The Golden Bench of God* had been met with rejection. Scribners had passed on this story too.

But Hurston was content in her cabin. For the next five years she paid attention to her dog Spot, a brown and white scruffy terrier. She painted the house, worked in her gardens, planting pink verbena plants around the palm trees, scattered with bright poppies. The plants, like her, ran wild.

In a letter to editor Burroughs Mitchell, Hurston describes the blue open sea. She calls the fish, crab, and shrimp brilliant jewels in the water. At night the tropical waters and breezes lapped and lulled her to sleep. Hurston loved living life close to the soil. She declared herself happier than she had been for at least ten years.

But the world around her was rapidly changing and for the better, for African Americans. In 1954, the United States Supreme Court ruled that segregated schools were unconstitutional. Most African Americans considered the *Brown vs. the Board of Education* decision a long overdue victory, but Hurston believed otherwise.

"If there are not adequate Negro schools in Florida, and there is some residual, some inherent and unchangeable quality in white schools, impossible to duplicate anywhere else, then I am the first to insist that Negro children of Florida be allowed to share this boon," Hurston wrote in an editorial in the newspaper the *Orlando Sentinel.* "But if there are adequate Negro schools and prepared instructors and instructions, then there is nothing different except the presence of white people. For this reason, I regard the ruling of the U.S. Supreme Court as insulting rather than honoring my race." Civil rights leaders denounced Hurston, while those favoring segregation wrote her fan mail. Again Hurston stood between two worlds.

She wrote constantly, but earned little for her efforts. She once pawned her typewriter for grocery money. Hurston's health also was worsening. From her trip to Honduras she had caught a "tropical fluke," as she said. Sometimes she had swellings in her arms and groin. She also had periodic gall bladder infections, from which she'd been suffering since the 1930s. Although Hurston had recovered from her depression, and loved her cabin, life was still a struggle—and she was still fighting it.

eight

Wrapped in Rainbows

y 1955 Hurston set out to tackle another immense project. Never one to think small, she planned to write the biography of Herod the Great, the ruler of the country of Judea in the first century BC. Encouraged by Scribners, Hurston wrote, "I am bunching my muscles for the leap" into another book. The subject quickly grew too extensive to handle without strict focus. In March Hurston's landlord sold her snug cabin from underneath her. Another blow came in August of 1955 when Scribner's rejected her manuscript about Herod.

Hurston temporarily landed on her feet again with a job as a librarian at Patrick Air Force Base in Cocoa, Florida. Hurston hated it, along with the salary of $1.88 an hour. After one year she left to find something else. But life grew increasingly difficult. Hurston was middle-aged, overweight, and sick. She had little energy and money to support her ambition.

Hurston moved to Merritt Island, across the Indian River from Cocoa. She lived in a house trailer, nursed a recently diagnosed stomach ulcer, and worked on revising her book on Herod. In the hot tropical climate she wrote and slapped away at mosquitoes. Money dwindled further and by October of 1957 she had moved to Fort Pierce, Florida to write for a local newspaper. She contributed articles to the *Fort Pierce Chronicle* for the next two years. Owner C. E. Bolen recalled that Hurston sometimes wasn't the easiest writer to work with. "She could cuss you out in a nice way, and you would never know what she was talking about," Bolen said. "She was something with those words."

Never satisfied with a job for long, in February of the next year Hurston started work as a substitute teacher. After befriending a local doctor, she boarded in his house. At Dr. C. C. Benton's she put in a vegetable garden, planted azaleas, and watched morning glories weave and twine their way around the yard. She entertained the local children by telling them her stories. By now Hurston weighed more than two hundred pounds. She had always loved to eat, especially ice cream.

Short of breath, tired, and suffering chest pains, Hurston was hospitalized in September of 1958 with heart disease and high blood pressure. Doctors sent her home with medication and told her to take better care of herself. Hurston needed to give up smoking and lose weight.

But her symptoms were too much. Her weight, combined with the "tropical fluke," heart and gall bladder problems, and a stomach ulcer, led to a stroke on October 12, 1959. Hurston, who had always been tough and driven, now was weak and unable to concentrate and care for herself. She entered St. Lucie County Welfare Home a few weeks later.

A 1958 photo of Hurston and two unidentified friends in Fort Pierce, Florida (*Courtesy of Zora Neale Hurston Collection, George A. Smathers Libraries, University of Florida, Department of Special Collections*)

On Thursday January 28, 1960, Zora Neale Hurston had another stroke and died at seven o'clock in the evening. Unlike her vibrant life, she died quietly. Her middle name was misspelled on her death certificate as Neil, and no one noticed.

But in death, as in life, Hurston refused to be forgotten. News of her death spread quickly. Donations for her funeral began to pour in from friends, family, publishers, and students. More than one hundred people attended her funeral, where Hurston was dressed in a bright pink gown with fuzzy pink high-heeled slippers on her feet. She was buried in the city's segregated cemetery, the Garden of the Heavenly Rest.

"Zora Neale went about and didn't care too much how she looked. Or what she said. Maybe people didn't think so much of that. But Zora Neale, every time she went about, had something to offer. She didn't come to you empty," said Bolen, owner of the *Fort Pierce Chronicle*, at the funeral.

Reverend Wayman A. Jennings commented, "They said she couldn't become a writer recognized by the world. But she did it. The Miami paper said she died poor. But she died rich. She did something."

Even Hurston's manuscript about Herod the Great continued on without her. One evening in February of 1960, a few days after Hurston's funeral, Patrick Duval, a sheriff's deputy, was driving past Hurston's former home. He noticed smoke rising from the backyard. He discovered that people had been hired to clean out the place and were burning Hurston's storage trunk of papers and manuscripts. Knowing who Hurston was, Duval quickly turned a garden hose on the trunk to put out the flames. He saved many of Hurston's papers, including the incomplete manuscript *The Life of Herod the Great*.

The rescued papers, although badly charred, were donated to the University of Florida's Department of Rare Books and Manuscripts.

For many years there was no marker for Hurston's grave. The exact whereabouts in the cemetery are unknown. However, Alice Walker, a fellow black author, erected a marker in 1973. The simple stone reads:

> Zora Neale Hurston
> "A Genius of the South"
> Novelist   Folklorist
> Anthropologist
> 1901   1960

In many ways Walker's tribute summarizes Hurston's life, even down to the dispute in her age. She was actually sixty-nine years old at the time of her death. Despite the times Hurston lived in, she had been an anthropologist, playwright, folklorist, novelist, activist, journalist, and teacher. Hurston wrote more than any black woman of her time. The author of seven books, she also wrote more than one hundred short stories, plays, essays, and articles. She was granted honorary degrees and spoke at major universities.

Hurston's gift of telling a good story was important to the Harlem Renaissance and her times. She believed that folklore and African American art were being trampled down by history. Her work with folklore showed her pride in the beauty, language, and tales of her race. She lived at the moment in time when many folklore traditions, rituals, and stories stood to go by the wayside, passing out of the hearts and memories of southern African Americans who migrated north. Instead, Hurston was there to preserve this precious culture. All of

The work of Zora Neale Hurston has shaped and influenced the writing of Pulitzer Prize-winning author, Alice Walker. *(Courtesy of AP Images)*

her life she strived to stop that casualty and was thrilled by the variety of the folklore she collected.

Hurston's mother once said that someone had sprinkled traveling dust on her doorstep the day Hurston was born. Lucy Hurston must have been right. In her thirty years as a writer, Hurston traveled from Florida to New York to Washington, D.C., to Haiti to Jamaica to Honduras. Each trip gave her another layer of texture to add to her writing. She brought these personal experiences into her stories and shared them with others. However difficult her life might have been, Hurston maintained her sense of self and individuality. Despite being constantly plagued with financial worries, Hurston steadfastly remained determined to eke out a living as a writer while living her life to the fullest.

"I have known the joy and pain of deep friendship. I have served and been served. I have made some good enemies for which I am not a bit sorry," Hurston wrote. "I have loved unselfishly and I have fondled hatred with the red-hot tongs of Hell. That's living."

timeline

1891   Born on January 7 in Notasulga, Alabama.

1904   Mother, Lucy Hurston, dies September 18.

1917   Attends Morgan Academy in Baltimore.

1918   Attends Howard Prep School in Washington, D.C.

1919-
1924   Attends Howard University.

1921   Publishes "John Redding Goes to Sea."

1924   *Opportunity* magazine publishes "Drenched in the Light."

1925   Short stories "Spunk" and "Color Struck" win second place in *Opportunity* magazine's literary contest; attends Barnard College and studies anthropology.

1926   Launches *Fire!!* magazine with other artists.

1927   Collects folklore in the South; marries Herbert Sheen on May 19; separate shortly after; publishes story about Cudjo Lewis in *Journal of Negro History;* Charlotte Osgood Mason becomes Zora's patron in mid-September.

1928	*World Tomorrow* magazine publishes "How it Feels to be Colored Me."
1929	Collects folklore in the Bahamas.
1931	Falls out with Langston Hughes over their opera *Mule Bone;* revue *The Great Day* performed in May; divorce from Sheen finalized July 7, 1931.
1932	Begins second folklore collecting trip in the South.
1933	Sister, Sarah Hurston, dies of pneumonia; *Story* magazine publishes "The Gilded Six-Bits" in August.
1933-1934	Works as a drama teacher at Bethune-Cookman College.
1934	*Jonah's Gourd Vine* published.
1935	*Mules and Men* published.
1937	Receives grant from the Guggenheim Memorial Foundation to study voudou and black culture; writes *Their Eyes Were Watching God;* novel published in the fall.
1938	*Tell My Horse* published.

1939   Marries Albert Price III on June 27; *Moses, Man of the Mountain* published.

1940   Separates from Price.

1942   *Dust Tracks on a Road* published.

1944   Marries James Howell Pitts on January 18; divorces eight months later.

1948   *Seraph on the Suwanee* published; charged with sexually molesting a young boy; indicted, then found innocent.

1950   *Negro Digest* publishes "What White Publishers Won't Print;" *American Legion Magazine* publishes "Why the Negro Won't Buy Communism."

1959   Suffers stroke on October 12; enters St. Lucie Welfare Home.

1960   Dies on January 28.

sources

CHAPTER ONE: Jumping at the Sun

p. 9, "peach hickories on it . . ." Zora Neale Hurston, *Dust Tracks on a Road* (New York: Harper Collins, 1996), 48.

p. 10, "No one around . . ." Valerie Boyd, *Wrapped in Rainbows: The Life of Zora Neale Hurston* (New York: Scribner, 2003), 14.

p. 10, "To her my . . ." Lucy Anne Hurston, *Speak So You Can Speak Again: The Life of Zora Neale Hurston* (New York: Doubleday, 2004), 8.

p. 11, "plenty more sons . . ." Boyd, *Wrapped in Rainbows*, 17.

p. 11, "cold conked," Robert E. Hemenway, *Zora Neale Hurston: A Literary Biography* (Urbana and Chicago, Illinois: University of Illinois Press, 1980), 14.

p. 11, "bales of cotton . . ." Mary E. Lyons, *Sorrow's Kitchen: The Life and Folklore of Zora Neale Hurston* (New York: Simon & Schuster, 1990), 2.

p. 11-12, "We had seen . . ." Boyd, *Wrapped in Rainbows*, 32.

p. 13, "suck sorrow for . . ." Hemenway, *Zora Neale Hurston: A Literary Biography,* 14.

p. 14, "No honest man . . ." R. Kent Rasmussen, *Farewell to Jim Crow: The Rise and Fall of Segregation in America* (New York: Facts on File, 1997), 116.

p. 16, "the one girl . . ." Hemenway, *Zora Neale Hurston: A Literary Biography,* 14.

p. 17, "jump at de . . ." Ibid.

p. 17, "It is my understanding . . ." Lyons, *Sorrow's Kitchen*, 2.

p. 18, "Zora is my . . ." Boyd, *Wrapped in Rainbows*, 28.

p. 18, "Don't you want . . ." Lyons, *Sorrow's Kitchen*, 3.

p. 20, "I was old . . ." Boyd, *Wrapped in Rainbows*, 45.

p. 20, "That hour began . . ." Hemenway, *Zora Neale Hurston: A Literary Biography,* 17.

p. 20, "I have often . . ." Boyd, *Wrapped in Rainbows*, 46.

p. 22, "the very day . . ." Ibid., 50.

p. 22, "Jacksonville made me . . ." Ibid.

p. 22, "I was deprived . . ." Ibid., 51.

p. 23, "I kept looking . . ." Ibid., 54-55.

p. 23, "I was shifted..." Lucy Anne Hurston, *Speak So You Can Speak Again: The Life of Zora Neale Hurston,* 12.

p. 24, "Poverty smells like . . ." Lyons, *Sorrow's Kitchen*, 23.

p. 24, "her father's house . . ." Ibid., 21.

p. 24, "She called me . . ." Zora Neale Hurston, *Dust Tracks on a Road,* 76.

p. 25, "There have been . . ." Boyd, *Wrapped in Rainbows*, 66.

p. 26, "hog-nosed, gator-faced . . ." Ibid., 71.

p. 28, "the empty holes . . ." Lyons, *Sorrow's Kitchen*, 24.

p. 28, "I had loosened . . ." Boyd, *Wrapped in Rainbows*, 72.

CHAPTER TWO: Drenched in the Light

p. 31, "This was my . . ." Boyd, *Wrapped in Rainbows*, 76.

p. 32, "And black men's . . ." Hemenway, *Zora Neale Hurston: A Literary Biography,* 36.

p. 33, "rough edged diamond," Ibid., 18.

p. 36, "I have a heart . . ." Boyd, *Wrapped in Rainbows*, 87.

p. 38, "I would like..." Zora Neale Hurston, *Spunk: The Selected Short Stories of Zora Neale Hurston* (Berkeley, California: Turtle Island Foundation, 1985), 18.

p. 39, "no job, no friends . . ." Boyd, *Wrapped in Rainbows*, 93.

CHAPTER THREE: Harlem and Hope

p. 44, "If my race . . ." Hemenway, *Zora Neale Hurston: A Literary Biography,* 29.

p. 44, "I'd rather be . . ." Ibid., 29.

p. 44, "was in love . . ." Ibid.

p. 45, "I had the same . . ." Lucy Anne Hurston, *Speak So You Can Speak Again: The Life of Zora Neale Hurston,* 15.

p. 45, "Most sincerely your . . ." Carla Kaplan, *Zora Neale Hurston: A Life in Letters* (New York: Doubleday, 2002), 465.

p. 45, "Devotedly, your pickaninny," Ibid., 223.

p. 45, "We wear the mask . . ." Boyd, *Wrapped in Rainbows,* 102.

p. 46, "shorthand . . . short of . . ." Hemenway, *Zora Neale Hurston: A Literary Biography*, 20.

p. 46, "the gift of . . ." Boyd, *Wrapped in Rainbows*, 100.

p. 49, "Almost before you . . ." Ibid., 95.

p. 49, "was certainly the . . ." Hemenway, *Zora Neale Hurston: A Literary Biography,* 36.

p. 49, "full of side-splitting . . ." Ibid.

p. 49, "I am just . . ." Ibid., 23.

p. 54, "when I set my hat . . ." Ibid., 31.

p. 54, "Caucasians stormed Harlem," Ibid., 27.

p. 54, "Who would think . . ." Ibid., 24.

p. 55, "a sincere friend . . ." Boyd, *Wrapped in Rainbows*, 126.

p. 57, "Youth speaks . . ." Hemenway, *Zora Neale Hurston: A Literary Biography*, 41-42.

p. 57, "a malicious, spiteful . . ." Ibid., 40.

p. 58, "The American Negro . . ." Rasmussen, *Farewell to Jim Crow: The Rise and Fall of Segregation in America*, 123.

p. 58, "I am not . . ." Hemenway, *Zora Neale Hurston: A Literary Biography*, 11.

p. 60, "more outlets for Negro fire," Ibid., 45.

p. 63, "Almost nobody else . . ." Boyd, *Wrapped in Rainbows*, 114.

CHAPTER FOUR: Traveling Dust

p. 66, "In folklore . . ." Lyons, *Sorrow's Kitchen: The Life and Folklore of Zora Neale Hurston*, 60.

p. 69, "could stomp a piano . . ." Hemenway, *Zora Neale Hurston: A Literary Biography*, 93.

p. 70, "The glamour of . . ." Ibid., 90.

p. 70, "We are charging home . . ." Boyd, *Wrapped in Rainbows: The Life of Zora Neale Hurston*, 152.

p. 73, "end of my . . ." Ibid., 156.

p. 73, "There she was . . ." Hemenway, *Zora Neale Hurston: A Literary Biography*, 106.

p. 73, "possessed the power to . . ." Boyd, *Wrapped in Rainbows*, 158.

p. 74, "I hear that . . ." Lucy Anne Hurston, *Speak So You Can Speak Again: The Life of Zora Neale Hurston*, 21.

p. 75, "get another stomach . . ." Lyons, *Sorrow's Kitchen*, 64.

p. 75, "pay night rocks . . ." Ibid., 65.

p. 75, "timid as an egg . . ." Ibid.

p. 76, "most gorgeous possibilities . . ." Hemenway, *Zora Neale Hurston: A Literary Biography,* 112.

p. 81, "beautiful and terrifying," Lyons, *Sorrow's Kitchen,* 73.

p. 81, "I don't know . . ." Ibid.

p. 82, "Not only can one . . ." Richard Wormser, *Growing Up in the Great Depression* (New York: Atheneum, 1994), 3.

p. 86, "Jeepers, creepers . . ." Edmund Lindop, *The Turbulent Thirties* (New York: Franklin Watts, 1970), 9.

p. 91, "I think it would . . ." Hemenway, *Zora Neale Hurston: A Literary Biography,* 145.

CHAPTER FIVE: Stories and Songs

p. 96, "The world wanted . . ." Hemenway, *Zora Neale Hurston: A Literary Biography,* 181.

p. 98, "I shall wrassle . . ." Ibid., 160.

p. 98, "new deal for America," Michael L. Cooper, *Dust to Eat: Drought and Depression in the 1930s* (New York: Clarion Books, 2004), 32.

p. 100, "the most gorgeous . . ." Boyd, *Wrapped in Rainbows: The Life of Zora Neale Hurston,* 278.

p. 101, "only half of me . . ." Hemenway, *Zora Neale Hurston: A Literary Biography,* 160.

p. 101, "Mind you, not . . ." Boyd, *Wrapped in Rainbows,* 246.

p. 102, "tore out of the place . . ." Hemenway, *Zora Neale Hurston: A Literary Biography,* 189.

p. 102, "most vital and original . . ." Lucy Anne Hurston, *Speak So You Can Speak Again: The Life of Zora Neale Hurston,* 22.

p. 104, "decided to abandon . . ." Hemenway, *Zora Neale Hurston: A Literary Biography,* 202.

p. 108, "I really wanted . . ." Boyd, *Wrapped in Rainbows* 274.

p. 108, "ultimate purpose as a student . . ." Ibid., 251.

p. 110, "We were really joyful . . ." Lyons, *Sorrow's Kitchen,* 77.

p. 111, "For a day and a night . . ." Ibid., 83.

p. 111, "The greatest power . . ." Ibid., 76.

CHAPTER SIX: Atop the Peaky Mountains

p. 115, "from the first to last . . ." Lucy Anne Hurston, *Speak So You Can Speak Again: The Life of Zora Neale Hurston,* 23.

p. 115, "sometimes I feel . . ." Boyd, *Wrapped in Rainbows,* 145.

p. 116, "cost you more . . ." Hemenway, *Zora Neale Hurston: A Literary Biography,* 250.

p. 116, "if science ever . . ." Lyons, *Sorrow's Kitchen,* 90.

p. 120, "Wherever the children . . ." Hemenway, *Zora Neale Hurston: A Literary Biography,* 258.

p. 120, "let my people go," Boyd, *Wrapped in Rainbows,* 330.

p. 123, "I did not want . . ." Hemenway, *Zora Neale Hurston: A Literary Biography,* 278.

p. 124, "I have been . . ." Boyd, *Wrapped in Rainbows,* 12.

CHAPTER SEVEN: In Sorrow's Kitchen

p. 130-131, "Please remember that . . ." Boyd, *Wrapped in Rainbows,* 385.

p. 132, "My country has . . ." Lyons, *Sorrow's Kitchen,* 109.

p. 133, "God keeps His . . ." Boyd, *Wrapped in Rainbows,* 401.

p. 133, "Day by day . . ." Ibid., 402.

p. 133, "Nagged by . . ." Ibid., 403.

p. 133, "For the first time . . ." Ibid., 404.

p. 133, "I was born with . . ." Ibid.

p. 135-136, "I have just not tried . . ." Ibid., 410.

p. 136-137, "If there are not . . ." Ibid., 423-424.

p. 137, "tropical fluke," Hemenway, *Zora Neale Hurston: A Literary Biography,* 342.

CHAPTER EIGHT: Wrapped in Rainbows

p. 138, "I am bunching . . ." Boyd, *Wrapped in Rainbows,* 413.

p. 139, "She could cuss . . ." Lyons, *Sorrow's Kitchen,* 111.

p. 141, "Zora Neale went about . . ." Hemenway, *Zora Neale Hurston: A Literary Biography,* 348.

p. 141, "They said she couldn't . . ." Ibid.

p. 144, "I have known the joy . . ." Boyd, *Wrapped in Rainbows,* 432.

bibliography

Boyd, Valerie. *Wrapped In Rainbows: The Life of Zora Neale Hurston*. New York: Scribner, 2004.

Bryant, Philip S. *Zora Neale Hurston*. Chicago, IL: Raintree, 2003.

Collier, Christopher, and James Lincoln Collier. *Reconstruction and the Rise of Jim Crow*. New York: Benchmark Books, 2000.

Cooper, Michael L. *Dust to Eat: Drought and Depression in the 1930s*. New York: Clarion Books, 2004.

Davis, Rod. *American Voudou: Journey Into a Hidden World*. Denton, Texas: University of North Texas Press, 1988.

Gates, Henry Louis, Jr., and K. A. Appiah, eds. *Zora Neal Hurston: Critical Perspectives Past and Present*. New York: Amistad Press, 1993.

Hemenway, Robert E. *Zora Neale Hurston: A Literary Biography*. Chicago, IL: University of Illinois Press, 1980.

Hurston, Lucy Anne and the estate of Zora Neale Hurston. *Speak, So You Can Speak Again*. New York: Doubleday, 2004.

Hurston, Zora Neale. *Dust Tracks on a Road: An Autobiography*. New York: Harper Perennial, 1996.

———*I Love Myself When I Am Laughing . . . and Then Again When I Am Looking Mean and Impressive*. New York: The Feminist Press, 1979.

———. *Mules and Men*. New York: Harper Perennial, 1990.

———. *Spunk: The Selected Short Stories of Zora Neale Hurston*. Berkeley, CA: Turtle Island Foundation, 1985.

————. *Their Eyes Were Watching God.* New York: Harper & Row, 1990.

Kaplan, Carla. *Zora Neale Hurston: A Life in Letters.* New York: Doubleday, 2002.

Lindop, Edmund. *The Turbulent Thirties.* New York: Franklin Watts, 1970.

Lyons, Mary E. *Sorrow's Kitchen: The Life and Folklore of Zora Neale Hurston.* New York: Aladdin Paperbacks, 1990.

Rasmussen, Kent. *Farewell to Jim Crow: The Rise and Fall of Segregation in America.* New York: Facts on File, 1997.

Stewart, Jeffrey C. *1001 Things Everyone Should Know About African American History.* New York: Doubleday, 1996.

Wormser, Richard. *Growing Up in the Great Depression.* New York: Atheneum, 1994.

Web sites

http://www.lkwdpl.org/wihohio/hurs-zor.htm
This Web site provides a good general biography.

http://www.floridamemory.com/Collections/folklife/sound_hurston.cfm
Sound recordings that Zora collected are featured on this Web site.

http://www.columbia.edu/cu/iraas/harlem/index.htm
Descriptions of Harlem, including its history, art, and politics can be found here.

http://www.zoranealehurstonfestival.com/newsite102004/aboutus.html
Readers interested in the annual festival held in Zora's name will find information on this site, as well as images of Eatonville.

index